JOYCE RUPP

CONSTANT
hope

Reflections and Meditations
to Strengthen the Spirit

**TWENTY-THIRD
PUBLICATIONS**
twentythirdpublications.com

TWENTY-THIRD PUBLICATIONS
One Montauk Avenue, Suite 200
New London, CT 06320
(860) 437-3012 or (800) 321-0411
www.twentythirdpublications.com

Cover photo: ©Shutterstock.com / Leigh Richardson

ISBN: 978-1-62785-347-7
Library of Congress Control Number: 2018959091
Printed in the U.S.A.

 A division of Bayard, Inc.

CONTENTS

LENT

EASTER TO PENTECOST

Feasts and Festivals

ORDINARY TIME

On you I depend from birth;
from my mother's womb
you are my strength;
constant has been my hope in you.

Psalm 71:6

Hope resides at the core of who we are. We have the ability to retain peace of mind and heart no matter how much thick gloom descends on our path of life. Our external world might be inundated with distress, but deep within us there abides a trust that God will see to our well-being in spite of evidence to the contrary. Psalm 71 declares that this vital quality has been rooted in us ever since we experienced the formative months in our mother's womb. How encouraging our life would be if we believed in this reality as we awaken to each new day.

We are meant to be hope-filled people. Yet the question looms large before us: Is it possible to have persistent hope when we live in a society where divisiveness and hostility doggedly work against this likelihood? Is it actually conceivable that we can foster an enduring hope, one that nurtures and sustains an unshakable peace no matter what our troubles might involve?

Maintaining an abiding confidence *is* possible, but the ability to preserve it does not come effortlessly. Time and again we will find it necessary to buoy up this virtue when difficult personal and world events press upon us. We will be asked repeatedly to place our hope in God, whom Psalm 71 refers to as our "rock of refuge" (v. 3).

We can be people of resiliency if we focus steadily on what enables our confidence to thrive: a relationship with the Holy One who dwells within us. This perpetual Love is boundless and abundant. In this sacred realm we find the grace and encouragement for hope to flourish. When we open ourselves to the resources of this Abiding Presence by setting aside time to absorb the insights and inspirations available to us, our hope grows in depth and consistency.

Prayer and meditation are some of the most valuable means for strengthening our resolve to carry hope with us wherever we go, however we are. Even so, the innumerable and continual distractions that plague our daily lives often challenge our desire to give ourselves adequately to this quiet time. The lack of solitude and silence easily leads to either forgetting or ignoring our vital relationship with God—where we renew and nourish our motivation to be peace-filled, hopeful persons.

RESTORING HOPE

The reflections contained in this book provide a source for keeping hope alive and steadfast. Each of these brief essays evolved from meditating on a Scripture text. These meditations come from my years of writing for *Living Faith*, a small magazine that offers a reflection on a Scripture passage from the daily Eucharistic liturgy. For each issue (which spans over a three-month period), I am assigned five days, with the option of choosing which of the Scripture texts for those liturgies I will use as the focus of the essay. Thus, you will find that some liturgical seasons have more reflections than others, and that only some of the feasts and festivals of the church year are included.

Because my writing assignments rest within the parameters of the prescribed Scriptures for a particular day, sometimes it takes much pondering to find something within those texts that speaks to my life and to the experience of *Living Faith*'s readers. Only through prayer and persistent reflection do insight and inspiration arrive. This has taught me the necessity and value of engaging the Scriptures silently to receive the message that the Holy One is ready to awaken in me.

I have also learned how open and patient I must be if I am to discover motivation and meaning through the biblical verses. Like you, I am absorbed in a culture that expects instant information and quick action. In order to gain the depth of Scripture, and not just skim across the surface, the discipline of slowing down internally and externally has to be practiced. From time to time, you will undoubtedly come across an essay in *Constant Hope* that leaves you puzzled, uninspired, or uninterested. I encourage you to then set the essay aside, focus on the Scripture verse at the top of the reflection, turn it over quietly in your mind and heart, and pray for what is meant to be revealed to you.

INTEGRATING THE MESSAGE INTO DAILY LIFE

These reflections include more than just "a nice thought" for encouragement. The contents are intended to be integrated into your mind, heart, and active life. In order to assist with this, I have suggested a question at the end of each essay. These questions invite you to pause before you leap into the day's activities. By responding to the questions, you have an opportunity to make a connection between the reflections and what is happening in your inner and outer world.

Before reading the essay, pause to be in the loving presence of the Holy One. Let the content of the reflection and the question tumble around in you for a while. Look for the correlation between the reflection and your personal situation. Then, take what you have gleaned with you to sustain your union with God and strengthen your resolve to live in a hope-filled way. May what you find and reflect upon within the pages of *Constant Hope* generate and encourage you to give the best of who you are for the benefit of both personal and global transformation.

The life and teachings of Jesus provide both motivation and encouragement for living with an enduring hope. Remembrance of the wisdom contained in the gospels helps us to grow steadily in trust and become ever more proficient in extending love as generously as Jesus did. Let us engage with life by being people of hope, assured of a strong bond with the Holy One who lifts us up when we are bent low, moves us forward when we are hesitant, and carries us gently when we are too weary to bear our cross alone. Let us keep our hope constant and bring to mind often this bold assurance: "Now hope that sees for itself is not hope. For who hopes for what one sees? But if we hope for what we do not see, we wait with endurance" (Romans 8:24–25).

ADVENT

A Promise of a Refreshing Future

Streams will burst forth in the desert, and rivers in the steppe.

Isaiah 35:6

While visiting in Arizona, I went hiking in the Sonoran desert. Having rarely been in that type of terrain, I fully expected to find only arid land with little or no water on the sandy landscape. Imagine my happy surprise when I came across several narrow ripples of water flowing down the creases of hillsides. The elation I felt at the sight of those small streams echoes Isaiah's message. The prophet promised a refreshing future to a people who lived in a state of despair. They could hardly imagine that the arid terrain of their lives might be blessed with a new spirit of peace and freedom. In today's world, with ever increasing violence and division, it is equally difficult to imagine a world where people live in harmony with one another. Yet, this dissension could change as quickly as the streams that are promised to "burst forth in the desert." This surprise could occur if more of society turned toward compassion and justice. Isaiah reminds us to not give up hope but to live in a way that promotes health and well-being for all who live on our planet.

How do you contribute to the promotion of justice and peace?

Always with Us

I have been with you wherever you went.

2 Samuel 7:9

These reassuring words spoken by the Holy One through the prophet Nathan to King David can readily be addressed to each of us. Never has there been a time when God failed to accompany our lives, even during those times when we did not have a felt sense of divine presence. This enduring relationship results from the gift of Jesus coming to dwell among us. He did not act like a tourist or guest and simply visit us for a brief period. He inserted himself as fully as possible into life on our planet. When Jesus departed from his human form, he left us his enriching presence in the Eucharist and sent his Spirit of Love to dwell within us as our guide. As we approach the celebration of the birth of Jesus, the Scripture readings keep assuring us that we are not alone. Advent is meant to wake us up to this wondrous reality, to turn our heart toward this Beloved Presence. Now is the time to make a deliberate effort to give our heart's full attention to our Eternal Companion who joins us on every step of the journey.

How will you choose to be aware of Christ's presence today?

Build Your House on Rock

"Everyone who listens to these words of mine and acts on them will be like a wise man who built his house on rock."

Matthew 7:24

On countless occasions I have read or heard something that prodded me to change an attitude or behavior so I would become more aligned to the teachings of Christ. And how many times I let that insistent urging sit there without acting on it, refusing "to build my house on rock." Nice thoughts are easy to entertain but difficult to carry into the solidity of action where they can make a difference. Good intentions remain just good intentions until they come alive in both attitude and deed. I recognized this a few months ago when I became acutely aware of my waning patience. Sure enough, it did not take long before I faced the choice of whether to build my house of kindness on a strong foundation or let it crumble away. I was with someone who tried my patience to the utmost. My first response was emotional—a desire to ignore the graced prompt to be kind. I wanted to show my irritation with a negative comment. Fortunately, patience won out. I relearned how difficult it is to move away from thinking of doing good deeds and actually putting them into practice.

What will help you to ensure that your house is built on rock?

Drawn Like a Magnet

Great crowds came to him.

Matthew 15:30

One thing we know for certain about Jesus from the gospel stories is that people of all sorts were drawn to him. He could be described as having "a magnetic personality." People came from everywhere to be in his presence. They sat on hillsides and stood in throngs for hours just to hear him talk. They were attracted to him for many reasons but most certainly because of the goodness they sensed in who he was. They obviously felt an inner stirring they could not explain and found surprising peace by listening to what he said. What about us? Are we drawn to the goodness and love Jesus brought into the world? Do we find ourselves moving toward the Holy One in a compelling way? The medieval mystic Mechtild of Magdeburg described herself as being drawn like a magnet to God. Our own experience may not be this powerful, but within each of us is the potential of immense attraction to this Great Love. During the Advent season, why not let our hearts be focused on Christ? Why not let our hearts be drawn like a magnet?

How will you let your heart be drawn to Christ?

9

Fruitfulness

"Blessed is
the fruit of
your womb."

Luke 1:42

For anyone who prays the Rosary or the Angelus, the words "blessed is the fruit of your womb" quickly become such a natural part of the prayer that one tends to say the words without much thought. Have you ever wondered why Elizabeth used the word "fruit" to refer to Mary's womb when she spoke of Jesus, rather than saying "blessed is the baby of your womb" or "blessed is the child"? Webster's Dictionary defines "fruit" as "the effect, result, or consequence" of something. Jesus was the fruitful consequence of Mary's faith after she responded positively to the invitation to bear God's beloved son. A piece of physical fruit usually contains a seed of some type within it. If the seed is planted and tended, this results in more fruit being produced. The child in Mary's womb contained the seed of divinity, a seed that grew in fruitfulness through Jesus' life and teachings. This fruit would result in untold numbers of followers coming to know and love God. No wonder Elizabeth cried out when she saw Mary, "Blessed is the fruit of your womb!"

How has the fruitfulness of Mary's womb made a difference in your life?

Gathering the Lambs

In his arms he gathers the lambs.

Isaiah 40:11

Watching airline passengers as they are welcomed by those who waited for their arrival is a sight that fills my heart with happiness. I sense the people's elation as they greet one another with hugs and kisses and wrap their arms around each other. What a precious experience to have someone be that glad about another person's presence. The prophet Isaiah speaks about this kind of welcome in reference to God's embrace. He reminds those in exile that God eagerly waits to greet and hold them closely, much like a shepherd lifting up a precious lamb or a parent cradling a newborn child. Jesus, too, uses this affectionate image to encourage his listeners to believe in a welcoming God. Advent opens the door for us to recall the Holy One's great love for humanity when Jesus came to live among us. Will we welcome Christ into our hearts in the same way that we are welcomed by the Holy One? Will we do so by greeting each person today with a similar kind of hospitality of heart, one that is considerate, friendly, and compassionate?

How will your hospitality of heart welcome others today?

Give Without Counting the Cost

Hardly a day goes by without someone reaching out to me with an unexpected kindness—a welcoming smile, a courtesy in a store, an affirming email message, a clarification for what I do not fully understand, a helping hand when carrying a heavy load, allowing my car into a line of traffic, offering a listening presence. None of these costs a cent to receive. All I need to do is graciously accept the simple yet generous act of kindness. Why, then, do I think I must have a sense of satisfaction for the kindness I give? The verse from Matthew's gospel leads me to pose some thought-provoking and uncomfortable questions: How eagerly and readily do I give without expecting recognition? How much of myself will I extend in order to benefit another? Do I expect gratitude from those whom I share considerable time assisting? How much moaning and groaning do I express when a situation requires the fullness of my attentive heart—when I know that the same fullness of attention will not be returned to me? Ultimately, the big question is: Am I willing to give without counting the cost?

Consider the questions above in the light of how you extend kindness.

God Is Faithful

God is faithful.

1 Corinthians 1:9

Last March heavily scheduled commitments pressed upon me. During the first week I decided to entrust every single thing I did into the Holy One's hands. I tried to engage with each event calmly. If a day necessitated "hurry up," I moved through it with the assurance of divine strength supporting me. When March ended, I looked back with gratitude, seeing how all had gone well. Peace kept a stronghold in me. As we move through Advent I recall how confidence in the power of divine presence kept me from feeling overwhelmed or falling into discouragement. God is always faithful, but I have to do my part so this love can assist me. For many who read this reflection, Advent will have a lot of "push and hurry." You will try to go slowly but cannot always do so. Sometimes you will have to speed up because of demanding tasks. When you cannot alter the pace, be sure to give yourself into the Faithful One's care. Receive the benefits of this beloved presence and whatever you are engaged in will most surely go better. Your peace will be sustained.

What will help you to entrust each part of your day into the Faithful One's care?

Heralding the Good News

Cry out at the top of your voice...herald of good news!

Isaiah 40:9

Isaiah encouraged people to keep the possibilities of social and spiritual renewal alive by their voice and their actions. I wonder what the good news might be that we can proclaim this Advent season. The daily newspaper and evening news certainly do not give much prospect of renewal. The troubles of the world lead us to feel hopeless until we turn within, to the place where the source of all hope resides. There we find the assistance of the Holy Spirit to help us view life differently. If we are quiet and attentive, reasons for hope will stir within us. We then gain an approach to life different from the one we hear about in the daily news. Then we can see and hear the positive aspects of life. Our awareness of the innate goodness of others becomes clearer. We are drawn to the beauty of nature as a reflection of the Creator. The Scriptures we read and the sacraments we receive move us toward love. Advent requires that we become still enough to uncover these hopeful dimensions for being heralds of good news. Let us give ourselves to regenerative silence.

How might you herald good news this Advent?

I Will Give You Rest

"Come to me all you who labor and are burdened, and I will give you rest."

Matthew 11:28

When I speak to groups about compassion, individuals will sometimes share how weary they are from their work or homecare that consists of tending infirm persons. If we are not in the situation of being a caregiver to someone ill, aged, or disabled, we might not know the daily demands and stresses these caregivers experience. Day after day they are asked to be present to mental, emotional, or physical needs and to do so with generous kindness and unending attentiveness. This grueling routine can eventually lead to exhaustion. The "rest" that Jesus promises to burdened caregivers most often comes through other people who understand and respond with thoughtful help when a caregiver's well-being requires a break. During this Advent season let's become aware of those who are weary and reach out to them. Discover what they might need from us to make their difficult tasks easier. How can we help lighten their load? If a friend cares for a sick or aged spouse, or a parent has a special-needs child, how can we alleviate that situation? Let's extend Christlike "rest" to others this Advent.

What might you do to extend "rest" to a weary one this Advent?

Listening Carefully

[Joseph]
did as the angel
of the Lord had
commanded
him.

Matthew 1:24

Joseph had an unsettling dream in which his sensibly made decisions got drastically upended. When he awoke, Joseph realized God was calling him to accept Mary with her pregnancy, even though Joseph previously thought the most compassionate response would be to quietly divorce her. Joseph listened to the divine envoy in his dream and said "yes" in spite of how it threw his life into the chaos of uncertainty. Mary also listened and responded positively when God's messenger visited her. Thus it came about that Jesus was born because both parents listened intently and heeded the voice of the Holy One. They accepted their challenging future, not because the messages made sense. Indeed, the messages were unexpected and strange. Rather, Mary and Joseph accepted with faith that which could not be understood. And isn't that how we, too, live our life? We trust in the Spirit's divine guidance, even though we may not understand how our life is to unfold. We, too, respond with faith when we sense we are being led in a direction we do not understand, but one that seems to be what God desires of us.

*What would enable you to listen intently
to God today?*

Recognizing Divine Presence

Ask for a sign from the Lord, your God.

Isaiah 7:11

God speaks to Ahaz, king of Judah, encouraging him to ask for a sign. This invitation hints that something wonderful awaits Ahaz if only he is willing to receive it. Ahaz does not ask for a sign, but God goes ahead and gives him one anyhow: a virgin shall bear a son and name him Immanuel. Ahaz is to be attentive and look for this sign. He is to carry hope that divinity will become visible through Immanuel, the name meaning "God with us." In these Advent days before the celebration of Christ's birth, let us take to heart the Holy One's request of Ahaz. Let us look for signs of where and how God moves in and through the common occurrences of our days. Let us seek this presence amid our hurried activities and in the calm moments at communal worship and personal prayer. Let us recognize God's graced movement in our own and others' kindnesses. Let us acknowledge the Holy One in the flickers of goodness that emanate from morning to evening both in those we love dearly and in those in whom we least expect to find this blessed presence.

Where will you look for signs of God's presence in your life today?

Naming Divinity

"And holy is his name."

Luke 1:49

An unusual development occurred when I began writing *Fragments of Your Ancient Name*, a book of reflections on each of 365 names for divinity. I started by composing a short comment on each name. By the time I wrote a dozen of these I noticed they had turned into prayers. I ought not to have been surprised. A name not only identifies someone; it immediately places us in a relationship. A name personalizes and connects us with the one we are designating. I learned that I could not just write *about* names for divinity, I was compelled to write *to* the One whose presence beckoned me. Each name implied an association of some kind, not just an objective description. How we designate divinity reveals how we think and relate to this Being. When Mary responds to Elizabeth with the Magnificat she proclaims: "*The Mighty One* has done great things for me." The title Mary chooses is one that designates her awareness of the tremendous influence the Holy One has on her life. Take time today to reflect on how you name divinity and what this implies about the relationship you have experienced.

What name most expresses your relationship with our divine being?

Never Give Up on Others

Lebanon shall be changed into an orchard.

Isaiah 29:17

When Isaiah speaks to a people caught up in self-indulgence, he reprimands them for being attentive to their personal cravings while remaining oblivious to a wounded and struggling society. Ironically, in the four weeks before Christmas, our culture also reflects Isaiah's era. Commercials and marketing ads urge us toward excessive self-indulgence by insisting we spend extravagantly. Isaiah never gave up on the people whom he coaxed to draw near to God. To show how convinced he was of the people's ability to change, Isaiah used the image of a wilderness transformed into a fruitful orchard. We ought never give up on ourselves or on others, either. It does no good to complain and gripe about the commercialism of this season. Our attitude and actions are what will make a difference. Each decision of ours to be a person of kindness in spite of our resistance will contribute to the spiritual orchard. Each choice to buy fewer items and care more about those who have less than we do will turn our hearts away from the barrage of "too much" and toward the fruitfulness of which Isaiah spoke.

How will you contribute to those who have less than you do?

Renewing My Hope

They that hope in the Lord will renew their strength.

Isaiah 40:31

In one of his homilies Pope Francis said, "If there is no hope, we are not Christian. That is why I like to say: do not allow yourselves to be robbed of hope." Hope-filled people inspire and boost the enthusiasm of others. With their spiritual roots sunk deep in Abiding Love, they can stand strong in the wild storms of life and not give up. Hope-filled persons reach out wide and far to receive this empowering strength that comes in many disguises. Jesus was a carrier of hope. We are meant to be the same. The world's suffering and lack of peace can challenge our confidence. During Advent the questions naturally arise: "Are we hope-filled? How do we keep this essential virtue alive?" Not by self-reliance alone. Isaiah reminds us that persons "who hope in the Lord" are the ones who renew their strength. We journey inward to find the Endless Source that feeds the river of love and goodness in our hearts. When we do so, we have the courage to continue hoping in spite of what appears dismal. This Advent, let us revive our hope.

Are you hope-filled? How will you keep hope alive this Advent?

Sustained by Divine Kindness

The Lord protects strangers; the fatherless and the widow he sustains.

Psalm 146:9

For those of us who have not experienced trauma such as being a refugee in a foreign land, an orphan without a family, a person living in a homeless shelter, or a widow in a financially deprived situation, the words of Psalm 146 might not impact us in the way they do someone who has struggled to stay alive amid ongoing deprivation. I thought of this as I listened to an immigrant describe her harrowing journey from a destitute life in a drug-terrorized country to eventually become a citizen of the USA. The speaker's description of the tearful farewell to her family members whom she might never see again, the utter fright of possible rape or a violent death when furtively leaving her country, the challenge of learning English and finding a job, all this helped me realize how this woman could truly comprehend Psalm 146:9 as her reality. God sustained her. She made it through her terrifying ordeal and eventually found peace in a country where she felt safe. This Advent, let us look at how the psalm's message applies to our own life, as well as to that of others.

When have you leaned heavily on divine kindness and strength?

The Waistband of Justice

Justice shall be the band around his waist.

Isaiah 11:5

When Isaiah prophesies about the coming of a Messianic King, he uses a fascinating metaphor to describe justice: a waistband. In past history, waistbands served various purposes, from a place to fasten items like knives or to attach jewelry and other personal decorations. Today, waistbands serve a practical purpose. If there is not a waistband around a pair of pants, they can slip down. In Isaiah's world, justice had been eliminated for the poor. Marginalized and mistreated persons cried out for someone to notice and assist them. When Jesus came as the one Isaiah prophesied, he certainly wore justice as a waistband. He reached out to those whose basic rights had been neglected or taken away. He taught his followers to have justice as a focal point of their lives. The questions I ask myself in Advent are these: Are "my pants falling down"? How strong is my waistband of justice? Will it hold up my values as a follower of Jesus, the Just One? Is my waistband strong enough for me to speak out and act on behalf of those who have no one to speak for them?

Respond to the questions that conclude this reflection.

LENT

Changing Hearts

I will forgive their evildoing and remember their sin no more.

Jeremiah 31:34

As often as I am reminded through the Scriptures that God is merciful and forgiving, it is still sometimes difficult to have that truth settle fully in me. What helps in accepting the merciful heart of divinity is seeing this goodness reflected in a human life such as that of Nelson Mandela. This past president of South Africa changed his attitude radically while he was imprisoned for twenty-seven years. Mandela entered his incarceration as an egotistical, high-powered leader of a rebel group that advocated an end to apartheid. While in prison, Mandela turned his heart around by recognizing the inherent goodness of each prisoner and guard. After finally being freed, Mandela gave his energy toward the social change needed in his country. He chose to be merciful, urging forgiveness and reconciliation with those who had caused violence and heartache for himself and his people. Doesn't this sound like a reflection of the voice of God given to us through the prophet Jeremiah? Doesn't this example call for a change of heart in any of us who still hold grudges and refuse to forgive those who have harmed us?

Are there any grudges in you that are waiting to be released?

Conditions for Discipleship

"The Son of Man must suffer greatly and be rejected by the elders."

Luke 9:22

The verse that follows Luke 9:22 contains a tough requirement for the followers of Jesus. After he speaks of his own death, Jesus goes on to say, "If anyone wishes to come after me, he must deny himself and take up his cross daily and follow me." Thus, Jesus sets the condition of discipleship. Not only will he be the one to suffer greatly, but those who choose to follow him must also be willing to accept the resultant consequences. They will not escape some type of hardship and pain in doing so. No wonder the disciples were not always enthused about accompanying Jesus. No wonder we are not always enthused, either. In our world today where divergent values and discordant opinions exist, challenges are bound to develop for those attempting to live the gospel teachings. The conditions for being a Christian lead to questions: How firm is my discipleship? What am I willing to experience for the sake of following Jesus? Will I endure rejection? Live simply? Respect all of life? Forgive seventy times seven? Eliminate harsh judgment of people different from myself? Give generously to those in need?

Spend time with one or more of the questions listed in the above reflection.

Drawn Aside

He took the twelve disciples aside by themselves.

Matthew 20:17

Would you be thrilled to be taken aside by Jesus to spend precious time learning from him? Actually, we have this opportunity every time we turn inward through prayer. In the same way Jesus took his disciples away from the crowds to teach them, so we are to spend time with him during Lent. It is there we will learn and be encouraged to embrace and live his teachings. During Lent we are invited to sit in the classroom of the gospels and intentionally pay closer attention to our beloved Teacher. We choose to be with him, to reawaken and integrate more of his beliefs and values. Lent is the perfect time to choose one of the four gospels, to read and reflect on a portion each day. If we do so, we will be much like the disciples, intently listening and gleaning the messages of Jesus. If we are Christian, it is imperative that we return again and again to the gospels. For it is there that we can be reinspired to live wholeheartedly the beautiful and challenging ways of the One who first drew his disciples aside.

How will you choose to be drawn aside to be with Jesus?

Finding What Has Been Lost

"He was lost and has been found."

Luke 15:32

In each of the three parables related by Jesus in Luke's fifteenth chapter, joy arises when that which has been lost is found, whether the lost one is a lamb, a precious coin, or a beloved child. So many things of our life need finding time and again: purpose in life, hunger for the Holy One, a sense of well-being, steadfast love, enthusiasm for life, the direction of our heart, trust in divine providence. The list could go on and on. What is quite astounding is that a part of us can be lost and we may not even know it is gone. In the roller coaster of endless activity and the constant information reaching us in our global world, this is not surprising. Lent encourages us to slow down, to give ourselves to a greater amount of reflection and quiet. In doing so, we will gradually discover what needs to find its way home. As we go seeking, it is good to remember that we do not do this alone. Always our divine Companion, who restores us to joy and wholeness, guides our way.

*What has been lost in your life
and awaits your calling it home?*

Forming Good Habits

**I, the Lord
alone, probe
the mind and
test the heart.**
Jeremiah 17:10

This past year I've grown in awareness of the "scenarios" that crowd and clutter my mind, those imaginary settings in which I conceive of what someone might be thinking, feeling, or planning to do. These mental scenarios waste a lot of energy that could be spent on something worthwhile, such as picturing justice and equality for our world. The more I intentionally send the negative mental imaginations and unloving judgments on their way, the more quickly I become alert to the next time they zoom into my mind. Each deliberate intention to cease negative thinking makes it easier to boot them out with an inner smile. When I do so, I say to myself, "Oh, here is my six thousand and five hundredth scenario." The word spoken to Jeremiah strengthens my resolve to cease this mental haranguing. I recognize that I have neither the ability nor the right to "probe the mind and test the heart" of another with my preoccupations of what they might or might not do. Lent provides the opportunity to be deliberate in forming good habits that can outdistance and delete our not-so-good ones.

*Is there a habit of yours
that needs changing?*

Harden Not Your Hearts

Harden not your hearts as at Meribah, as in the day of Massah in the desert.

Psalm 95:8

Meribah and Massah received their names during the Exodus. Meribah means "quarreling" and Massah, "testing." These places were named for the Israelites, who grumbled a lot as they made their way through the wilderness. First it was about not having their kind of food. This time it was about the lack of water. Moses responded by scolding them for testing God's providence. This only incited the people more and they threatened to kill Moses. He passionately petitioned God, who then supplied the water they needed. Regrettably, when we murmur about our less-than-satisfactory situations, Moses is not around to intercede. A bit of complaining can be helpful. A lot of it is harmful. I get my complaints out by writing in my journal, grumbling to myself when I go for a walk, or talking to my spiritual director. This keeps me from continuing my inner griping endlessly. To prolong it would definitely harden my heart. When I stop complaining and open up to the presence of the Holy One, I do not always receive "water" like the Israelites, but I do obtain the ability to let go and live more peacefully.

What enables you to move beyond your times of complaint?

Kinship with Jesus

I gave my back to those who beat me, my cheeks to those who plucked my beard.

Isaiah 50:6

The Suffering Servant in the Book of Isaiah aptly describes the suffering that Jesus endured in his last days: fear, humiliation, intense suffering of body and spirit. Jesus endured all of this. Because he was fully human he did not escape the struggle that comes with intense suffering (Hebrews 2:14–18). During his agony in the garden, such extreme dread takes over Jesus that he sweats blood. He realizes that his crucifixion and death will soon come by those waiting to destroy him. Out of this terror, Jesus goes to his disciples to ask them to watch with him. Imagine the humility it took to do this. Here he is, their strong and wise teacher, their calm in the storm. They look to him for strength, and now he comes in great need, asking for their strengthening support. Only after an excruciating struggle to have his suffering on the cross taken away does Jesus turn his entire self in surrender to his Abba. Knowing this, we can find kinship with Jesus when we go through our own suffering. We have a companion who has been there before us.

In what areas of your life do you find kinship with Jesus?

Lenten Sackcloth

And all of them, great and small, put on sackcloth.

Jonah 3:5

The people of Nineveh repented of their wayward life by donning sackcloth and ashes. In the time of Jonah, sackcloth was usually made from coarse, black goat hair. You can imagine how uncomfortable and itchy the repenting people felt when wearing it, similar to how a rough wool sweater feels on our skin. Each movement would remind them of their decision to repent. Today it is not external clothes that indicate repentance. What counts is the change taking place in the inner sanctum of the heart. Our ego clutches tightly to harmful thoughts, words, and deeds that gradually become ingrained in us. Our efforts to rid ourselves of these wayward aspects of self can leave our spirit feeling scratchy and uncomfortable. In this time of Lent our external observances are meant to direct us to this inner realm where true transformation takes place, no matter how "itchy" we feel. If we want to see signs of repentance we look and listen to how we are thinking, speaking, and acting. We discover whether or not we are truly repentant within these dimensions of our lives.

What uncomfortable sackcloth are you wearing this Lent?

Let Us Set Things Right

Come now, let us set things right, says the Lord.

Isaiah 1:18

Lent provides a focus and an avenue for us to "set things right." And what might those "things" be? Much depends upon our personal situation but the issue of *priorities* undoubtedly tops the list for many of us regarding what may have gotten out of sync. It may be that we need to review and reset our time for prayer or restore significant relationships that have been upended by allowing work or some self-oriented ambition to take precedence. Setting things right could mean realigning a connection with another by engaging in reconciliation, or pulling back into place those thoughts that judge others or that draw one away from a moral life. If we are unsure about what might need setting straight in our life we can respond to the following questions: What has led me to deter from my desire to be my best self? Who or what has tumbled from my heart either by choice or by unawareness? Have I strayed from my intention to live my faith well? Is the path from my heart to the heart of Christ a straight and steady one?

Choose one of the questions above to ponder in regard to setting things right.

Love Pours Into and Out of Hearts

The love of God has been poured out into our hearts through the Holy Spirit.

Romans 5:5

Poured. That word indicates flowing, moving, entering a container of some kind. Have you ever poured liquid into a cup or glass and it accidentally overflowed? If so, you know how fast the liquid spreads over the area where the container stands. In Romans 5:5 what is being poured forth is divine love, a compassionate and unconditional gift that never stops filling the container. And the vessel into which it is being poured is our very own heart. What an exquisite image to carry with us as we move through our Lenten days, especially if those days hold people or situations that divert our attention away from peacefulness. What would happen if we paused and recalled this verse of Scripture and the image of God's love flowing into us when we are frustrated, discouraged, anxious, or angry? What would happen if we envisioned this same Love overflowing the container of our hearts and spreading to others? When we remember that we are vessels of divine love, we are drawn back to our best self where kindness, patience, hope, understanding, and forgiveness reside. Then our love can spill over into the lives of others.

How does Ever-flowing Love spill over from your heart into the lives of others?

Observing Carefully

Observe them carefully.

Deuteronomy 4:6

In Deuteronomy, Moses urges the people to observe "the statutes and decrees" of God. To "observe" indicates vigilance, to pay attention to what is required, to notice a specific type of response and act accordingly. I recognize in my life what a necessity this awareness is. The question is not that of wondering what is expected from the teachings of Scripture if I am to be a follower of Jesus. It is more a question of how conscious I am of what I am doing or not doing, thinking or not thinking, feeling or not feeling, in relation to those teachings. The key word of Moses' directive regarding observation is the word "carefully." When I went to a thesaurus to look for words equal to this term I found among them the following: "sensibly, prudently, judiciously, cautiously, consciously, wisely, vigilantly." Each one of these substitutions applies fittingly to how we are to observe the statutes of the Hebrew and Christian Scriptures, especially the two great commandments of loving God and loving others as ourselves. Each descriptive word formulates an entire meditation for our use.

In what specific way will you live God's decrees "carefully" today?

Protection for Our Hearts

For he has strengthened the bars of your gates.

Psalm 147:13

Psalm 147 praises God for being a guardian of the people by strengthening the gates leading into Jerusalem. These gates allowed entry for all who arrived. They had to be sturdy in order to provide safety for those who lived within the city. If the gates were durable enough, their enemies would not be able to break through and get inside to harm the occupants. Our hearts are like the city in this psalm. They also need strong gates of protection so they will not be invaded by what could bring harm. We ought not close our hearts off from others, but we must also be careful about what enters in. We have to be vigilant in our fortification against resentments and hurts that try to leap through the gates and destroy our desire to forgive. Selfishness and lack of gratitude rust and weaken the inner gates. Our heart relies on spiritual safeguards to resist the voice of our culture telling us to stake our happiness solely on material things. Daily prayer and vigilant attention strengthen the sturdy, inner gates and help keep the enemies from breaking through them.

How do you protect the gates of your heart?

Reversals and Returns

"For they have become depraved."

Exodus 32:7

It is difficult to imagine the Exodus people stooping so low as to worship a golden calf. They were freed from the bondage of Egypt, given sufficient nourishment for the journey, guided along the way, and continually forgiven by God for their stiff-necked ways. Yet in a situation of extreme stress and anxious uncertainty they returned to doing something they thought they left behind in their beliefs and behavior. The dictionary defines "depraved" as "to make morally bad, leading into bad habits." I do not like considering the possibility that I, too, could "become depraved." In taking a closer look, however, it becomes obvious that I do return to behaviors I thought I left behind. I say, "I'm not going to act that way again." (Then I do.) "I'm not going to think those negative thoughts anymore." (But then I think them.) "I am going to be nice to her." (But I am not.) Instead of judging others for their *depravity*, I benefit much more from recalling my own reversals. This humbling process leads me to return to good choices and behavior with a forgiving God by my side.

What sort of reversals do you experience?

Serving Christ in One Another

"What you did not do for one of these least little ones, you did not do for me."

Matthew 25:45

Regrets. Most of us have them. When I consider the wrongs I have done, I see more omissions than deliberate actions that caused them. Even now, I can pass by someone in need, only to realize a mile down the road that they could have used my help. I can be inordinately occupied with my own interests and forget to make that phone call to check on someone grieving or ask how healing is developing for a patient recovering from surgery. There have been times when a relative longed for a listening heart and I rambled on and on about some issue of no relevance whatsoever. At other times, I failed by not writing to Congress to urge their concern for the vulnerable ones of our society. In our current self-absorbed culture it is remarkably easy to avoid reaching out to those who need our caring presence. In the meantime, people who are impoverished, imprisoned, hungry, sick, without shelter, mentally ill, or stuck in refugee camps miss the gift that could be theirs if we would choose to reach out and serve Christ in them.

How might you serve Christ in someone who could benefit from your attention?

Singing a Love Song

Listen to my voice.

Jeremiah 7:23

I was sitting on the porch writing. Not far from me a little house finch perched on a branch. I heard the bird warbling a glorious tune, but I did not bother to listen, my focus being elsewhere. Eventually, I thought, "Listen to this beautiful song. It is too lovely to miss." When I looked up, I saw the male finch singing to a female finch sitting at the feeder. She was busy grooming her little toes and pecking at the food. She paid absolutely no attention to the vibrant singing. Finally, she just up and flew away. The other bird's song stopped instantly, realizing his fervent desire to move her heart had been in vain. God is always singing a love song to me, desiring to get my attention, wanting me to know how much I am cherished. But I get absorbed in things that distract me. Like the little finch, I ignore and miss the loving voice, oblivious to the beauty of the divine song and the One who sings it. Had I not been graced to pause and listen that day, I would have missed this crucial reminder.

When is the last time that you paused to listen to God's love song to you?

When Guilt Is Good

My sacrifice, O God, is a contrite spirit.

Psalm 51:19

There is a tendency in our culture today to think that guilt is always an unhealthy emotion. Guilt is most certainly not of value when it produces an adverse effect on our spiritual growth by crushing us with a false belief of our unworthiness, or when it shames us into believing we are a bad person. Contrary to what many believe, however, guilt is not always an inadequate response to wayward behavior. Guilt becomes beneficial by moving us toward necessary contrition. Victor Parachin describes this in his article "When Guilt is Good." In a society where many tend to either dismiss or to blame others for their own wrongdoings, he states that guilt can move us to "accept responsibility for our actions." Parachin also suggests other benefits from a sense of guilt. It can prompt us to extend an apology and make amends, develop humility by recognizing our own character defects, as well as heal hurt and anger when we acknowledge our remorse. We are never too old to have a healthy sense of guilt because it can lead us to be contrite for our misdeeds.

Have you experienced any benefits from "feeling guilty"?

The Power of the Tongue

The tongue is a small member and yet has great pretensions.

James 3:5

People refer to the tongue to describe a variety of human behaviors, such as tongue-lashing, tongue-tied, tongue-in-cheek, and tongue twister. James also refers to the tongue when he writes to the early Christians. He uses clever metaphors to describe how something as small as the human tongue can wield vast power. He points out how a tiny flame can start a huge fire and how the small bit in a horse's mouth controls the strong animal. Then James comments on how we humans have a choice in how we use our tongue: "From the same mouth come blessing and cursing" (3:10). Think of the divisiveness that escalates from just one negative comment. Think, too, of how a voiced affirmation elicits a person's sense of well-being. A while ago I read a wise adage that urged everyone who speaks about another to first ask three questions: "Is it true? Is it kind? Is it necessary?" Only if the response is "yes" to all three questions should the person then continue speaking. If more people really followed this teaching there would be a lot more blessed silence in our world and a definite increase in kindliness.

What kind of messages will your tongue speak today?

Throwing Stones

So they picked up stones to throw at him.

John 8:59

A few countries still allow their citizens to stone to death someone accused of a serious crime. In most countries, citizens would never approve of this heinous deed. Nevertheless, people *do* throw stones. Rather than physical stones, they throw verbal ones. They do so by the way they speak and act toward those whom they consider strange or radically different, judging them guilty by not measuring up to cultural standards. Society's "undesirable ones" are stoned with hostile and prejudicial comments. Think of descriptive words hurled at people whose lifestyle is dysfunctional or who dress shabbily and reek of body odor; consider stones thrown at transgendered persons or at those with mental illness who exhibit odd behaviors, or who have a disease like Tourette Syndrome, which is manifested by involuntary tics and loud, verbal utterances. Descriptions such as "weird, freak, worthless, loser, idiot, scumbag" and other cruel labels damage the spirit in the same way that hard stones damage physically. Each negative remark becomes a projectile thrown at the body of Christ. As we renew our efforts to be Christlike, let us be intentional about putting down any stones we carry.

Have you ever thrown stones at others? If so, what were some of those stones?

Unbinding Our Heart

They had weighed him down with fetters, and he was bound with chains.

Psalm 105:18

The jealous brothers of Joseph bound him with chains and weighted him down before they threw him into a well where they presumed he could not escape. Joseph's fetters symbolize the parts of our self that hinder our inner freedom. They keep us weighted down in attitudes and behavior that restrain our growth, preventing us from loving as fully as we could. What might those restraining obstacles be? The list includes a lot of possibilities, including always needing to be right, constant self-pity or self-doubt, blaming others instead of taking responsibility, endless criticism, refusal to leave the painful past behind, happiness at another's misery, continual fretting and worrying, arrogant putdowns and haughty opinions, an ungrateful heart, avoiding forgiveness, and thinking only of self. Whatever keeps us from being at peace and from accessing our innate goodness—this will be what chains and holds us captive. Lent focuses on breaking these fetters, on freeing us to be people of deep and lasting love. It is time to sever the shackles that bind our hearts and thwart us from activating our spiritual potential.

What fetters keep you spiritually captive?

EASTER TO
PENTECOST

A Place of Prayer

> **We went outside the city gate along the river where we thought there would be a place of prayer.**
>
> *Acts 16:13*

Paul traveled constantly to preach. He was faithful to prayer even though he was away from home and not able to be in his usual routine. We may not be traveling far from our home, like Paul, but we are usually on our way to some place every day, even if it is just to the mailbox or the backyard. Whether we are going to a doctor's appointment, out to the garden or to the office, bringing children to school, or engaged in some other form of movement, we each have an opportunity to pause and unite with God. We can always find a place to pray. For Paul it happened to be along a river. I often pray in the airport or in the car. (I call my car "a little hermitage on wheels." It serves me well as a place of prayer.) There's no excuse for just floating through the days without a "hello" to God because I am en route somewhere. All I need to do is turn my heart toward this Beloved One and be intentional about making the inner connection.

What works best for you in finding a place of prayer during the day?

A Time to Get Up and Go

The angel of the Lord spoke to Philip, "Get up..." So he got up and set out.

Acts 8:26–27

In the Bible God often urges people to "get up and set out." Prophets are called to go forth and proclaim the Holy One's message. Joseph hears, "Get up. Take Mary and the child into Egypt." Jesus tells those who are healed to "get up" and live fully. When Philip moves on, he does so without knowing why until he comes to the Ethiopian eunuch who is struggling to understand Christ's message. Because Philip went as he was told, he realizes he had been sent to address the Ethiopian's religious questions. To "get up" implies action. Every day the Spirit encourages us to act for the benefit of our own spiritual growth or that of others. It is much easier to focus on an electronic device, watch television, remain absorbed in an intriguing book, or be caught up in household errands than to get up and go where we can lend a helping hand or a compassionate heart. We might not even have to leave our house. Perhaps the call is to go and pray, or to notice others in our midst who will benefit from our kindness.

Is now the time for you to "get up and go"?

45

Difficult Departures

> **"But now, compelled by the Spirit, I am going to Jerusalem."**
>
> *Acts 20:22*

Before Paul left the city of Ephesus he gave a touching farewell speech, acknowledging that he would most probably never see the people again. This announcement landed a hard blow on their hearts. Paul's presence and preaching had changed their lives. They were a supportive community for him and he, in turn, grew in his fondness for them. How their hearts must have ached to see him go. ("They were all weeping loudly as they threw their arms around Paul and kissed him" [Acts 20:37].) Like Paul, some people today sense that same Spirit urging them to make decisions that impinge on the lives of those whom they love and who will greatly miss them. Men and women leave cherished family and friends to live as missionaries in foreign lands; some enter cloistered monasteries with limited visitation; medical personnel join Doctors without Borders in dangerous situations; social workers go to help in refugee camps; military personnel depart for long sojourns as peacekeepers. Let us pray for strength and safety for all who follow where the Spirit leads them and for those who weep at their departure.

How have you responded to difficult departures, either your own or others'?

Easter Grace

"We are witnesses of these things."

Acts 5:32

When Peter and the apostles are accused of continuing to preach in Jesus' name, Peter explains that they cannot help but act in this way because of the amazing power of God's Spirit moving through them. On the days when I am attentive to how this Spirit moves in my life I also experience this grace-filled reality. Things happen that I neither plan nor cause. I marvel at how the Spirit of the Risen Christ stirs and inspires through incidents like the following: A woman described a dream of her young, recently deceased husband; this dream led her to go into his office library where she always sensed his presence; there she found the very book that helped her with her acute grief. In another incident, a nurse told me how he was unable to overcome his negative judgments of a colleague until a simple phrase he read helped him do so. Then there was a postal worker who reconciled with a daughter who surprisingly turned toward him after years of being away. These revelations renew my conviction to be attentive to how Easter grace comes alive in each of us.

When have you witnessed the effectiveness of Easter grace?

Essential Goodness

He was a good man.

Acts 11:24

We know when we are in the presence of a good man or woman. There is something about their demeanor—how they look at people with openness and their way of approaching others—that shows genuine respect and integrity. We know they "walk their talk." We like being with them. Their presence leaves us wanting to emulate them in our attitudes and behavior. We learn today that Barnabas was a generous, thoughtful, affirming, and kindhearted individual. He is described as being "filled with the Holy Spirit and faith." We catch glimpses of why Barnabas was known to be "a good man." He recognizes and affirms the goodness of those around him. We are told that he praises the people for their faith and encourages them. We also learn how generous Barnabas is with his time and abilities. He selflessly leaves his own successful work to go to Tarsus, look for Saul, and bring him back to teach because he knows Saul will inspire the people to live their faith more fully. Let us be grateful today for the good people who touch and inspire our lives.

What qualities of goodness most attract you to others?

Extending a Welcome

When they arrived in Jerusalem, they were welcomed by the church.

Acts 15:4

The local community greeted Paul and Barnabas warmly when they came to Jerusalem. That same sort of welcome is not always the case in our churches. "Welcome" involves a lot more than a greeter at the front door saying "Good morning." That is a start at hospitality but it does not absolve the rest of us from being friendly and acting like we are glad to be sharing the pew with others. I have been a stranger in churches where not one person smiled at me. We are probably not even aware of how cliquish we can be. Because we feel comfortable and it does not require much effort, we tend to greet those we know and ignore those we do not. A smile and a friendly "hello" go a long way in letting others sense we are glad they are present. Author Denis Waitley writes, "A smile is the light in your window that tells others there is a caring, sharing person inside." Observe yourself the next time you go to church. Notice if you smile and who gets the benefit of that caring gesture on your face.

When is the last time you greeted a stranger at church?

I Will Not Leave You Orphans

"I will not leave you orphans; I will come to you."

John 14:18

The disciples probably did not understand what Jesus meant about feeling orphaned until they stood at a distance from his cross on Calvary and watched with terror as he died in crucified agony. Perhaps only then did the reality of his death plunge into their hearts and leave them feeling forsaken. This emotional response led them to turn from his death and go into hiding because they realized he had truly departed from them. They must have questioned his not leaving them orphaned because of having visibly witnessed his last breath. We know from the gospel narratives that the disciples came to believe the truth of this promise when Jesus appeared to them in his risen form. Like the disciples, an orphaned feeling takes over us at certain times. We, too, may wonder if our Trusted Companion has left us on our own. When we feel forsaken, this is the time to recall Jesus' words, "I will not leave you orphans." This gives us the opportunity for our faith to grow stronger, to trust with all our heart that we will also come to experience an "Easter Sunday."

When have you felt "orphaned" from the Risen One's presence?

In You We Live and Move

> "For 'in him we live and move and have our being,' as even some of your poets have said."
>
> *Acts 17:28*

This rich statement encompasses the core of my relationship with the Holy One. My faith receives inspiration from the thought of being enfolded, surrounded, and intertwined with this beloved presence. All of who I am, each part of what my life involves, has a connection with my Creator. I was so taken with the beauty of this reality that many years ago I developed a chant based on Acts 17:28: "In you we live and move. In you we have our being. In you we shall remain. In you is our abiding." This verse sustains me in times of uncertainty and fretfulness. Sometimes I sing it out loud and sometimes I hum it quietly. At other times, I simply let it quietly circle my mind and heart. When I remember how closely united I am with the Holy One, I am able to surrender my hesitations and worries. This verse also prompts me to turn away from what lures me into self-centeredness. Because it is in God that I "live and move and have my being," I am motivated to give my all to the One in whose love I exist.

In what ways will you unite with the Holy One today?

Life Beyond Death

"You will grieve, but your grief will become joy."

John 16:20

Before Jesus was forced to take up his cross and walk to his death on Calvary, he spoke a reassuring message to his disciples: "Your grief will become joy." I wonder if his words comforted or left them bewildered. When suffering has visited me during various types of losses it has left me bereft of joy. Only after going through a period of grieving and gradual surrender to what cannot be changed does joy reappear. Oftentimes it does not return in the same form, but a lifting of sorrow does occur. I have come to trust in the hope contained in the reassuring words of Jesus. The accounts of his resurrection also provide a strong foundation for this belief. New life does follow death, but it takes faith to count on something unknown and valuable being possible after significant loss occurs. This belief is a strong Christian message. Much depends on our attitude and response to suffering. Patience is essential, along with keeping one's heart on the hope inlaid in the resurrection. Future peace and joy return, but only after grief and acceptance have been given their due.

How have you experienced "life beyond death" after significant loss occurred?

Lydia Moments

**Lydia...
listened...
and the Lord
opened her
heart.**

Acts 16:14

Paul preaches about Jesus. Lydia listens. Her heart opens as she hears Paul speak. God moves through her spirit and she proceeds to ask for baptism. Listening, opening, receiving—these are big steps to spiritual growth. That is not the end of the story. Next comes an equally important one: bringing faith into action. Lydia has looked inward. Now she looks outward and immediately extends hospitality. She opens her home and insists that Paul and Silas stay with her. Lydia's example challenges me. I like the inner response I feel when a message of spiritual growth moves me toward greater love of the Holy One. However, I don't always feel as positive when I am then called to go outward to someone needing my time and attentiveness. For example, in my morning meditation I may have uplifting thoughts and feelings about Jesus the Healer. Then the day unfolds, and I get a phone call. It requires leaving the work I am doing to focus my attention on listening to a person whose life involves health issues. That's a "Lydia moment," an opportunity for my spiritual growth to become visible.

What have you learned through the "Lydia moments" in your life?

Not Ready to Hear

**"I have much
more to tell
you, but you
cannot bear
it now."**

John 16:12

When Jesus speaks lovingly to his friends in his farewell address, he implies there is much the disciples still need to hear and understand, but they are not ready for it. He then assures them that when the Spirit comes, they will be able to perceive in a new light what took place. This gift arrived after the disciples entered into the suffering and death of Jesus and received the grace of Pentecost. Only then did they have the capacity to grasp the significance of the painful event, to understand it in the retrospect of the resurrection. In many ways, this is also true of our lives. We yearn to understand our personal journeys, but the deeper meaning of our life experience often reveals itself only after we have passed through the tough times. Only then do we comprehend how the event graced us with growth in our faith. Life will always hold some unwanted event that can teach us more about who we are. Suffering can gift us with insight and compassion if we patiently wait for the Spirit to reveal it to us.

*What are you not yet ready
to hear or understand?*

Serve with Gladness

Serve the Lord with gladness.

Psalm 100:2

Each of us is called to "serve the Lord" in some way, no matter what our situation might be. Whether we are youthful or aged, limited by illness or actively engaged, we can share the gift of our presence in some positive way. We serve the Holy One by how we serve others because God dwells within all of us. It never ceases to surprise me how little it takes to bring joy into another person's life. Oftentimes our service is not some action we take as much as it is the attitude we have toward others. If we do choose an action, this might consist of small deeds, something simple like smiling genuinely when we would prefer a sigh of exasperation, or pausing to listen to someone else's problems rather than continue to speak about our own. If we respond to others "with gladness" instead of self-oriented gratification, we are extending the kind of spirit that the psalmist encourages. When we start feeling grumpy, full of resentment or constantly annoyed, it is time to see if we are serving with gladness or mainly trying to fulfill duty and obligation.

How will you serve with gladness today?

Someone Greater Than Ourselves

God is greater than our hearts and knows everything.

1 John 3:20

One thing we humans insist on having is control. (Well, at least I do.) That's not a terrible thing. Our human nature requires a certain amount of security in order to bring our best to others. But when the going gets tough and the path to peace dissolves, control of our life usually gets wobbly, no matter how much we try to keep everything in order as we have planned. That's when it's time to remember this verse from John's letter. When we are not sure about trusting what is going on in our tumbled life, when we are hesitant to follow the truest link to our inner core of goodness, it is time to turn to the One greater than our own hearts. This wise Spirit who guides us to what is life-giving *does* know more than we do. We might not like to admit this when we are invaded by overwhelming distress and grasping onto the thinnest straw of calmness. But it's extremely comforting to know Someone wiser than ourselves will help us find the way to regain inner peace. If we just let go.

What happens to your trust level when your life goes awry?

Surprising Transformations

When he [Saul] arrived in Jerusalem he tried to join the disciples, but they were all afraid of him, not believing that he was a disciple.

Acts 9:26

Paul's surprising conversion altered him from a zealous killer into an ardent disciple of Christ. Such a radical change of heart seemed impossible because he had been totally convinced of his efforts to eradicate the Christians. No wonder the disciples questioned whether Paul really had a change of mind and heart. Their fear surfaced from a natural inclination to be hesitant in trusting such a significant difference. A similar disbelief occurs today when men and women return from transforming experiences such as a profound spiritual-growth retreat, a recovery program for addiction, or a challenging pilgrimage. When these experiences alter someone significantly, these persons return home with a desire to live differently, knowing they are no longer the people they used to be. However, these transformed individuals may find that those who knew their past will doubt the authenticity of their change. The story of Paul serves as a reminder to not give up believing in the power of divine love to transform someone's life, and for us to welcome them wholeheartedly when they return as "a new person."

Have you had an experience that changed you significantly?

Tended with Love

> "I am the true vine and my Father is the vine grower."
>
> *John 15:5*

Some years ago I walked through northern Spain during a season when the vineyards swelled with ripened fruit. The scene of such beauty and abundance was magnificent to behold. One day I passed by a field where an elderly man stooped over the vines, carefully tending the soon-to-be-harvested grapes. The vineyard keeper's concern for the grapes moved me deeply. He gently lifted each bunch of grapes and cradled them in his hand for inspection. Seeing him that conscientious about his work told me how much the man cared for the produce and the quality of what he was growing. That image turned my thoughts toward the teaching of the vine and the branches in John's gospel. I reflected on how the Holy One approaches us with a similar tenderness, holding us carefully, hoping that our good works will bear abundant fruit, and touching our lives with affection as we ripen into fuller love. In this Easter season, what joy we have in knowing we are cared for with attentive tenderness by the Risen Christ who is ever with us. Let us find renewed confidence from this intimate union.

When have you experienced God's attentive care?

The Memory Keeper

The holy Spirit...will... remind you of all that I told you.

John 14:26

Have you ever thought about the Holy Spirit as a memory carrier? Indeed, it seems this is what Jesus described when speaking to his disciples before his death. He told them an Advocate (a supporter, an encourager) would be sent to teach them everything they needed to know. This Advocate would remind them of what he had communicated to them so they could keep those teachings alive. We have this same Memory Keeper with us today. As nice as it sounds to have this wonderful reminder of the gospel principles, I do not always like to heed the memory prompts I receive. Just when I am ready to make a snide comment about someone who grates on my nerves, I get this inner counsel about being kind. When I want to ignore someone who will probably talk "forever" about her problems, along comes Memory Keeper prompting me to be generous with the gift of my listening. Fortunately, the Holy Spirit does not give up on any of us but keeps on sending messages that reflect what Jesus lived and taught. It is up to us to heed those reminders.

What will help you listen to the Memory Keeper's reminders?

FEASTS
AND
FESTIVALS

Love Bestowed on Us

Most Holy Name of Jesus ▪ *January 3*

> **Beloved, we are God's children now; what we shall be has not yet been revealed.**
>
> *1 John 3:2*

In *Someone Knows My Name*, a novel on slavery by Lawrence Hill, a stirring scene takes place in the bowels of a slave ship. A young, frightened girl who has been stolen from her tribe makes her way through the foul-smelling, totally dark place to take water to men and women who are chained together. She thinks she recognizes a boy from her village and calls out his name. In that brief moment his heart leaps with joy because someone acknowledges his presence. The boy's response indicates the power a name holds. In our era of uncertainty and insecurity, when we voice the name of Jesus, we recall how his time on Earth revealed the enduring love of divinity. John's letter echoes this, assuring us that we are "children of God," welcomed by a caring parent. Most of us seldom have a felt sense or a continual recognition of this intimate bond. Like the people of John's time we, too, need constant reminders and assurances of God's love "bestowed on us" (1 John 3:1). We may not fully know this gift, but that does not lessen the reality of the relationship.

How have you known the love God has bestowed on you?

Selfless Commitment to Love

Presentation of the Lord ▪ *February 2*

He took him into his arms.

Luke 2:28

When Mary and Joseph went to the temple to present their son for a blessing, this event promised to be a joyful one. Imagine the change of emotional tone when the elderly Simeon took young Jesus into his arms and spoke alarming words, ones that predicted the fierce heartache the mother of this precious child would experience because of what Jesus would suffer in the future. Think of the Pietà, that poignant visual of Mary receiving the dead body of her murdered child after she stood long hours beneath his cross. The feast of the Presentation boldly proclaims that faithful love requires selfless commitment. When we enter the realm of love, painful consequences may result. When Mary heard Simeon's prediction, it must have shaken her soul with dread, but she did not withdraw her love. If anything, her resolve to cherish her child grew stronger. Like Mary, we may be led into untold grief because of the affection we bear for another. If our love is strong enough, we will stand by their cross with the same abiding compassion that led Mary to stand by her son.

How have you been called upon to activate your selfless commitment to love?

The Faithfulness of St. Joseph

St. Joseph • *March 19*

"My kindness
is established
forever."

Psalm 89:3

This psalm illustrates God's faithfulness and kindness. The psalmist repeats each of the supportive qualities five or six times throughout the prayer. These reassuring words suggest strength, trust, constancy, and loving care. Not surprisingly, this psalm is chosen for the feast of St. Joseph, husband of Mary of Nazareth. His goodness reflects the central qualities of divine faithfulness and caring expressed in the psalm. We see Joseph's kindheartedness when he looked out for Mary's welfare rather than for his own reputation and well-being, taking the pregnant Mary into his home. He is there for Mary when she gives birth. Joseph's deep concern for his wife and child compels him to follow the warning given by God's messenger in a dream, to hasten from their homeland in order to protect his family from harm. Joseph is faithful. He is there for Mary in joy and in travail. In each scriptural account about Joseph we see him as a faithful, generous-hearted man. His choices and actions remind us that we, too, are meant to reflect these qualities in our lives.

What qualities of Joseph do you most admire?

Being a Christ-bearer

The Annunciation • *March 25*

"May it be done to me according to your word."

Luke 1:38

How did Mary manage to say "yes"? How did she find it possible to make a radical turn in direction? I try to put myself in Mary's place and feel what she felt, to think what she thought. What a startling and abrupt interference with how she believed her quiet life was going to evolve. The angel Gabriel certainly helped by assurance and support as this young woman pondered the possible consequences. Our "yes" to being Christbearers implies that we, too, need our "angels" if we are to respond positively. These people do not give up on us as we sort our way through our own challenging invitations, such as: Will you be a presence of compassion in required caregiving? Will you be a patient friend who listens to an endlessly repeated story? Will you be a church leader amid a culture that resists the gospel teachings? Will you be a forgiving sibling? Will you be kind to marginalized people? Each day is an "annunciation"—an invitation from the same Great Love who invited Mary to be a Christ-bearer. Now it is our turn. Will we also answer "yes"?

What challenges do you face in being a Christ-bearer?

God Is Our Strength

Visitation of the Blessed Virgin Mary • May 31

My strength and my courage is the Lord.

Isaiah 12:2

Recently I received a touching note from a woman whose husband has Alzheimer's. She described not only how painful it is for her to see the continual diminishment of her husband, but also how wearying and burdensome the endless details are that accompany this disease as she strives to care for him. She ended her note by assuring me she has every confidence she can get through this because she knows God will be her reservoir of strength. That statement touched me deeply. On this day when we celebrate the Visitation, Mary and Elizabeth's personal histories remind us to trust in this divine empowerment. Neither one of them found life easy—one too old and the other too young to bear a child. These women of faith encourage us to face our most disrupting situations with a similar attitude. If we try to go through our struggles alone, we will limp along with faint inner support. But when we lean on the Holy One who promises to be there for us, we find we have what we need to go forward and face the tasks at hand.

What part of your life is most in need of strength?

The Body of Christ

Most Holy Body and Blood of Christ

The bread that we break, is it not a participation in the body of Christ?

1 Corinthians 10:16

When my elementary school teacher prepared me to receive my first Holy Communion, she instilled in my young heart a reverence for receiving the Eucharist. She emphasized keeping my eyes lowered and to not look around at other people. She encouraged me to focus totally on being united with Jesus because she wanted me to be "in communion" with the divine presence. While I value this teaching, I also find another approach to be equally inspiring and prayerful. This approach also draws me into union with the Holy One. Before or after receiving the Eucharist, I look with love at those in the communion line. I marvel at the variety of people moving forward—each one being a beloved person embraced in the heart of God. I look at the diversity of faces, the varied shapes of body, the colors of clothing, and the diverse manner of walking. I think, "We are the body of Christ united in our reception of the Eucharist, joined interiorly with this Great Love dwelling within us all. No matter how different we each appear on the surface, the Eucharist gathers us into an unbroken unity."

How do you experience being a part of the body of Christ?

Encountering the Mystery of Divinity

Most Holy Trinity

> **Having come down in a cloud, the Lord stood with him there and proclaimed his name.**
>
> *Exodus 34:5*

On this feast of The Most Holy Trinity we meet the mystery of divine essence. Moses goes alone to Mt. Sinai, heeding God's counsel to be unaccompanied. Even "the flocks and herds are not to go grazing" where he is standing (Exodus 34:3). Imagine the ethereal atmosphere of this scene: the mountain is fogged in, and only objects extremely close can be identified. Moses sees little beyond himself, which must have left him feeling both vulnerable to danger and insecure about how to proceed. Suddenly, Moses knows he is no longer alone. His name resounds in the air. This follows with the most amazing proclamation by the visiting Presence, a description of divinity that dissipates Moses' fear and astounds his faith: "a merciful and gracious God, slow to anger and rich in kindness and fidelity" (v. 6). In that moment Moses knows he has met the Holy One and instinctively bows "to the ground in worship" (v. 8). As we enter into Moses' experience on this feast, let us, too, bow reverently in our hearts, acknowledging the love and mystery found in this Holy One who is near to us.

What have you learned about divine presence during the foggy times of your life?

A Heart Filled with Love for Us

Most Sacred Heart of Jesus

We have come to know and to believe in the love God has for us.

1 John 4:16

The image of a heart has long been used as an expression of love. This feast of The Most Sacred Heart of Jesus leads us to remember the fullness of love in Christ—the overflowing compassion and selfless dedication that poured forth continually from his presence. I have observed the power of this image to inspire and restore a valuable relationship with Jesus, particularly in two individuals separated from church participation for years. Both persons, each in their own time, found in the Sacred Heart an enduring tenderness that called them back home to their religious faith. Not everyone resonates readily with this image and, yet the love portrayed in it ought not be ignored. Questions arrive as we celebrate this feast of divine love. Have we "come to know and believe in the love God has for us"? Is there anything in our mind or heart that prevents us from accepting what this beloved heart of Christ offers? If so, how might we open the door to this gift? What do we hope to find as we ponder the Sacred Heart of Jesus? How can we increase our love?

Ponder some of the questions raised in this reflection.

God's Welcoming Arms

Nativity of John the Baptist • June 24

Truly you have formed my inmost being.

Psalm 139:13

John the Baptist is most remembered as the loud-shouting prophet who prepared the way for his cousin Jesus. We forget John was once a vulnerable newborn. Imagine what it was like when Elizabeth birthed this long-awaited child. She must have been thrilled to hold this tiny baby in her arms for the first time. As she cradled John, counting his fingers and toes, did she wonder who this child would be, how his life would unfold? In her song "Little One," Sara Thomsen sings directly to a newborn: "Oh, running, dancing child, May your heart stay free and wild." John's heart certainly followed this direction. His journey took him onto paths that undoubtedly worried and alarmed his aging mother. All parents can identify with both Elizabeth's marvel at her newborn and the concerns she would have as her child grew and matured. In each situation, so much trust in God is required. Each of us, whether we have children or not, can give our concerns for those we dearly love into the welcoming arms of the Creator who holds each person near to heart.

Is there someone today whom you will entrust into God's welcoming arms?

Transparency

Saints Michael, Gabriel, and Raphael • September 29

> "Here is a true Israelite. There is no duplicity in him."
>
> *John 1:47*

On this feast of the three angels, the liturgical readings invite us to reflect on their transparency and pureness. Artists often depict these qualities by painting angels with large wings and white clothing. Jesus described the transparency of his disciple, Nathaniel, with affirming words by saying that he had "no duplicity in him." In other words, Jesus recognized Nathaniel as a person who was neither deceitful nor disloyal. This disciple, whose name means "gift of God," possessed integrity. Jesus was saying that he saw no difference between who Nathaniel was and how he acted. Author Parker Palmer describes this kind of person as someone "who is the same on stage as behind stage." What a refreshing reminder of how true a person can be. The affirmation that Jesus gives Nathaniel takes us beyond our current culture where it is now difficult to discern what is real from what is fake, where lying is increasingly an acceptable mode of behavior, and duplicity is tolerated when it paves the way to being financially successful. Nevertheless, let us never stop believing in the possibility of "a Nathaniel" within each of us.

How does your life express integrity and transparency?

Father, Forgive Them

Our Lady of the Rosary ▪ *October 7*

But the Lord asked, "Have you reason to be angry?"

Jonah 4:4

Jonah counted on God's wrath to be thrust upon the Ninevites for their evil deeds. Instead, the people repented and the Merciful One forgave them. When Jonah fumed and insisted the people be punished, God asked him: "Have you reason to be angry?" Jonah's desire for revenge— "You go get 'em, God"—isn't that the quick response in many a human heart? Sometimes, no matter how often someone apologizes for a great hurt done, there's a part of us that seeks retaliation. We want them "to get what they deserve," some harsh action that "makes them pay for it." While justice needs to be meted out for those who commit grievous crimes, if we look to the story of God's pardoning the Ninevites, or to the words of Jesus on the cross—"Father, forgive them"—there is no doubt that our desire for revenge has to be replaced by an attitude of mercy. On this feast of Our Lady of the Rosary, we are reminded in our prayer to her that all of us need God's mercy: "Holy Mary, Mother of God, pray for us sinners."

Where does mercy reside in your spirit of forgiveness?

The Power of Remembrance

All Saints Day ▪ *November 1*

What we shall be has not yet been revealed.

1 John 3:2

In her book *The Mystery of Death*, theologian Dorothee Söelle writes: "These days of November...make me remember. They send me to the cemetery, at least inwardly. They make me aware that I am not the giver of my own life. Into the cloak of my life is woven all the affection and tenderness of the people who are no longer here and whom I remember."

These poignant lines give me courage regarding my future death. They remind me that I embody the potential of those positive qualities that lived in the deceased people I loved and who loved me. All Saints Day urges us to have hope even though the future "has not yet been revealed." We do not know how or when our death will be, but we do know the strengthening blessings we received from those who once journeyed with us. Remembrance of how they lived and influenced us by their goodness gives us the courageous resolve to live our life well. Thus, we will be prepared for our death. As we celebrate this feast, let us be grateful for those who shared their presence with us.

Who among your deceased loved ones inspires you to share your best qualities?

73

Never Far from Us

All Souls Day, Commemoration of All the Faithful Departed ▪ *November 2*

> Their passing away was thought an affliction and their going forth from us, utter destruction. But they are in peace.
>
> *Wisdom 3:2*

On my mother's birthday I led a retreat at a St. Scholastica Retreat Center, where we joined the monastery community for the Eucharistic liturgy. As I sat there, I found myself missing her presence even though she died seventeen years earlier. As a quiet sadness visited me, something inside pulled my attention upward. I looked up to see a beautiful stained-glass window above the pew where I sat. I felt instant amazement. Could it be? I looked more closely to be sure of what I was seeing. There above me stood a figure on the window that was depicted as St. Hilda. My mother's name was Hilda. Could it have been mere coincidence when I chose that particular pew? I think not. I believe our loved ones' presence is near to us and their love never ceases. If the faithful departed had the ability to come back and speak to us, surely they would want most of all to assure us of their peace and their desire for our happiness. Perhaps my mother's spirit influenced my turning to see the window so my sorrow could be changed into peace-filled joy.

Have you ever sensed the nearness of your deceased ancestors?

The Gift of Peace

Christmas, Nativity of the Lord • *December 25*

His dominion is vast and forever peaceful.

Isaiah 9:6

On this Christmas day, let us turn inward for a moment to remember Immanuel, who desires to have a loving allegiance in our relationship. This is not a ruthless ruler determined to force us into being fearful followers. Rather, this divine monarch rules our hearts with eternal tenderness and unconditional love. In this soul-space, we welcome divine Peace forever available to us. This accessibility generates a joy-filled spirit of gratitude. No matter how lonely or sad we might feel, no matter how much divisiveness exists within our family, no matter how extensive the violence in our world, let us open wide and receive the expansiveness of an Incarnate Love that knows no bounds. For within this peace and love resides all we need to commemorate the day with harmony. Nothing can rob our inner space of true serenity unless we allow it to be taken from us. Nothing can keep us from rejoicing in this beloved presence unless we close ourselves off. What a magnanimous gift offered to us from Immanuel, who came to dwell among us. How can we refuse such a marvelous present?

What response to the birth of Immanuel most resounds in your heart?

Courage to Speak

St. Stephen ▪ *December 26*

"Do not worry about how you are to speak or what you are to say."

Matthew 10:19

Soon after we celebrate Christmas, the church reminds us that we are to be disciples of Jesus. The feast of St. Stephen, the early Christian who courageously spoke of his faith, carries a potent message: do not be afraid to speak when it will benefit others. Our message may not be direct preaching like Stephen's was. Our words of discipleship might be ones of comfort, assurance, or guidance. When I am concerned about what to say to another, or worried about the value of my message, I tend to thrust my *self* into the center of the picture first, instead of focusing on the person(s) to whom I am speaking. Valuable energy can be spent by hesitating about what to say to grieving ones, to troubled individuals, or to someone who could benefit from our honesty or forgiveness. The words we speak make a significant difference because we bring with them a caring presence that speaks of God's love. Each of us can count on the Spirit to provide us with the words we need, just as Jesus promised his disciples when he sent them forth.

In what situations do you most need the courage to speak?

Speaking about the Beloved Friend

St. John, apostle and evangelist ▪ *December 27*

**What we have
seen and heard
we proclaim
now to you.**

1 John 1:3

John the apostle longed to tell others about
Jesus, his close friend and mentor. How deeply
John loved Jesus. His whole life revolved around
this relationship. There is little doubt regarding
John's growing appreciation of Jesus as he traveled and learned from this teacher and as he
observed his mentor's constant compassion for
wounded people. John shared many intimate
moments with Jesus. He was there during the
awe-inspiring transfiguration on the mountain.
It was this disciple who leaned against his friend
at the Last Supper, and John who endured heartache as he stood faithfully beneath the cross
on Calvary. So close was John to Jesus that he
received the great privilege of caring for Jesus'
grieving mother. John's heart raced as fast as his
feet when he ran furiously to see if the tomb was
empty after Mary Magdalene announced the
news. No wonder John tried repeatedly to tell
others about Jesus. He wanted everyone to know
and appreciate the Beloved who totally claimed
his heart. Imagine what can happen if, like John,
we spend significant time with the life and teachings of this treasured Friend.

*How would you describe your friendship
with Jesus?*

Loud Lamentation

Feast of the Holy Innocents ▪ *December 28*

> **A voice was heard in Ramah, sobbing and loud lamentation.**
>
> *Matthew 2:18*

Imagine the overwhelming grief that consumed the people of Bethlehem and its vicinity when their little boys were massacred by Herod. The searing pain of this uncontainable loss expressed itself in cries of communal lamentation. We do not have to look far in our own time to know of other *Holy Innocents*. Children like those at Sandy Hook Elementary School lose their lives to a deadly shooting. Boys and girls are kidnapped from their villages by warlords and forced to be gun-toting soldiers or turned into terrorists. Everywhere children are trafficked and used as sex slaves. Young ones fear for their lives when they carry contraband pressed on them by drug kings. In every country, children are paying for adult crime and indifference by being exploited and assaulted. What can we do? We can support organizations that work to change systems and structures that cause harm to children. We can mentor a child in need, reach out and help a stressed family in the neighborhood or parish, and always, we can join in compassionate prayer for the battered and bruised children of our world.

How will you help to support children in need of care?

ORDINARY
TIME

A Kind Mouth

**A kind mouth
multiplies
friends, and
gracious
lips prompt
friendly
greetings.**

Sirach 6:5

How much good and how much harm can come from the "mouth." I remember from years past some valuable one-liners individuals spoke to me in situations when I was in definite need of consolation and support, such as, "You have more strength than you realize," and "I know you can do this." Those few words were enough to help me move beyond my self-doubts and hesitations. I also remember the quips that left painful welts on my heart and served to diminish self-esteem: "If you don't like it in this community you can leave," and "You think you're better than everybody else." Gossip, derisive name-calling, bitter sarcasm, backbiting, ridicule—these and other hurtful jabs proceed from the mouth, but they find their source much deeper. They surge upward and out the mouth from mental and emotional movements that disregard or lack awareness of how each person bears the Spirit of Christ within them. Oh, that our mouth would always speak "friendly greetings" and bring to others an awareness of their core goodness by what we choose to say, or not say.

*How have the negative or positive quips
of others affected you?*

A Prayer of Protection

Our soul waits for the Lord, who is our help and our shield.

Psalm 33:20

One of the prayers attributed to St. Patrick is known as "the breastplate prayer." The name for this prayer of protection suggests the kind of defensive armor worn by the warriors of Patrick's era. Instead of metal armor, however, this Irish saint believed the presence of Christ to be his safeguarding shield, a defense from harm to body, mind, and spirit: "Christ be before me, behind me, above me, below me, around me, and within me." Some people find this prayer of surrounding one's self with divine presence to be of tremendous help when they are besieged by fear, danger, or any form of temptation. They use it for a shield of courage to ward off thoughts that torment with memories of past wrongs, as a guard against emotional entanglements that threaten an ability to make choices and decisions clearly, as armor from absorption of the harsh tirade of another's words and all-consuming suspicions, from possible physical harm in dangerous storms and persistent personal behaviors that cause distress to self and others, or from anything else depriving them of peace of mind and heart.

What part of your life needs St. Patrick's prayer for protection?

A Reason to Rejoice

"Rejoice with me because I have found the coin that I lost."

Luke 15:9

When my friend called to tell me how she lost one of her expensive hearing aids, it sounded similar to the parable of the lost coin. Diane described how she took care of five or six errands one afternoon as she drove from one shop to another. During that time she placed her hearing aids in her pocket, and when she came home she realized one of them was missing. In a state of panic, Diane hurried back to each place. She spoke to every clerk who waited on her and retraced the steps she had taken. Her voice held such jubilation and gratitude as she related the moment of actually finding the tiny hearing aid lying on a concrete parking lot. How astounding that she ever found it. No wonder Jesus used a story of losing and finding something valued to describe the joy God has over "one sinner who repents" (Luke 15:10). When I hesitate to let go of an old hurt or avoid repenting of my wrongdoings, I hope the memory of my friend's enthusiastic discovery will help me give the Holy One a reason to rejoice.

What precious virtue do you need to search for and recover in your spiritual life?

A Simple Touch

[Jesus] stretched out his hand, touched him, and said, "I will do it. Be made clean."

Matthew 8:3

Jesus could have cured the leper without stretching out his hand and touching the bodily wounds. A few words or even a look from Jesus could have healed the disease. The physical movement of touching the man created a strengthening connection between the Healer and the one being healed. The kindness of the outstretched hand of Jesus reminds me of the Sign of Peace that we are invited to share at the Eucharistic liturgy. For some, this ritual is an insignificant, and sometimes unwanted, gesture. I recognize this by the lack of eye contact, the slight pressure of a handshake, the barely audible murmur. For others, their extended hand speaks of openhearted kindness. I see warmth in their eyes and hear it in their voices. I sense their genuine offer of peace in the firmness of their hand touching mine. I don't suppose many of us consider ourselves as Christ extending healing to someone hurting when we offer the Sign of Peace. But if we could see into the minds and hearts of those we touch we might be surprised to know how much healing our simple gesture has elicited.

What happens within your spirit when someone extends the Sign of Peace to you?

A Spiritual Homeland

> I will plant them upon their own ground; never again shall they be plucked from the land I have given them.
>
> *Amos 9:15*

Ever since I was young I have tended to be a "homebody." When I am away from my residence for a week or more I feel relief and satisfaction as I reenter the space that welcomes me back. Whether I say "ah!" out loud or just feel it inside myself, I rejoice in the pleasure of being in "home territory." How much greater the joy of the people forced from their homeland to hear these words of God through the mouth of the prophet Amos. To "pluck" means to quickly remove something. These people had been forced to quickly leave their beloved homeland. They naturally resonated with the metaphor of being on their own land where they belonged. "Homeland" indicated a sanctuary of security, where familiar and friendly faces offered an immediate sense of hospitality. When we establish a solid relationship with God, our interior homeland resonates with these welcoming qualities. We are assured that we will not "be plucked" from this spiritual refuge. No matter what happens exteriorly, we can return repeatedly to the homeland of our heart where the Holy One resides.

How have you experienced God as your "homeland"?

A Radical Shift in the New Year

"New wine is poured into fresh wineskins."

Mark 2:22

The vast majority of people do not use wineskins anymore. Now wine is stored in bottles, jugs, or boxes. Today Jesus might say, "Stop gluing the cracks in a bottle or patching the box with duct tape." Actually, if we tried to do this, the wine would still probably seep through the bottle or the box. What a good image Jesus uses to make the point that true change involves a radical shift away from what has been. We can't keep patching old ways of behavior or duct-taping unsavory attitudes. There's a tendency to do the wineskin approach: "I know I said I'd pray every morning but it's too hard; I'll pray every other morning. I thought I'd be kinder to so-and-so but I'll try to avoid him, instead. Even though my resolution was to not gossip at all, I won't do it quite as often." When we fall into the "wineskin mode," our good resolutions slip away until we are back in old behaviors and attitudes again. Is it time to throw the glue and duct tape away and make a radical shift?

How would you answer the question that ends this reflection?

Be Mindful of Prisoners

Be mindful of prisoners as if sharing their imprisonment ...for you also are in the body.
Hebrews 13:3

The author of the Letter to the Hebrews urges us to treat each person as part of the body of Christ. We are to be "mindful of prisoners" as if we ourselves were incarcerated with them. There are many basically good people in prison who have hurt others by their poor choices and hard-hearted decisions. It is easy to judge them as "worthless" or "rotten," but we do not know what the early lives of these men and women lacked in comparison to ours, nor do we know what happened in their mind and heart to lead them astray. This does not mean that we condone their crimes or deny the need for justice. However, no matter what crime someone committed, each continues to be a human being filled with the same divine presence that inhabits us, even if that presence is heavily disguised. If we are not able to visit someone incarcerated, we can correspond with them. This communication allows us a way to enter their situation and begin to know them as human beings.

Have you found a way to be mindful of others?

Being Generous with My Presence

Greet Prisca and Aquila, my co-workers in Christ Jesus, who risked their necks for my life.

Romans 16:3–4

Prisca (also called Priscilla) and Aquila were first-century lay missionaries who accompanied Paul on his travels. Biblical commentaries do not tell us how this married couple risked their lives for Paul, but his praise of them indicates an exceptional dedication. He was obviously grateful for the extreme efforts they had taken as they accompanied him in his travels. I wonder if I am ready to *risk my neck* for the sake of another. Could I be that loyal and other-centered? Am I generous with my commitment and life? These questions lead me to ponder how dedicated I am to the well-being of others and how ready I am to give my full attention to those in want. I must constantly consider these aspects because society pulls me toward individualism and self-orientation. Placing others' concerns before my own, going the extra mile, doing without something I enjoy, allowing myself to be uncomfortable or inconvenienced, risking my reputation to stand up for someone unjustly accused or maligned, these are small but significant actions that enable me to *risk my neck* for the sake of another.

Is there anything that causes you to hesitate in being generous with your presence?

Calling Forth Our Gifts

Moses had laid his hands upon him.

Deuteronomy 34:9

Before Moses died, he laid his hands upon Joshua who was then "filled with the spirit of wisdom" and became the new leader of the people (Deuteronomy 34:9a). Moses recognized Joshua's abilities for leadership and expected him to take over his position. Like Joshua, we each contain innate giftedness. Oftentimes this latent ability stays hidden and has to be called forth from us in order for it to be birthed. Parents encourage children to face their hesitations and affirm their talents. Pastoral staffs call forth gifts by inviting volunteers to accept responsibilities in the congregation. Friends inspire one another to set foot onto the terrain of a new job. If we look at our personal history we will see that someone like a grandparent, teacher, pastor, colleague, confidant, spiritual director, perhaps even a stranger, believed in us when we did not believe in ourselves. These people, like Moses with Joshua, laid their hand upon us and blessed us by their affirmation and nurturing challenge. Let us be grateful for how the Spirit of God moved through those who were our "Moses" and enlivened our talents.

Is there a "Moses" in your life for whom you are grateful?

Carrying Others to Christ

At sunset all who had people sick with various diseases brought them to him.

Luke 4:40

Luke does not tell us that the sick came to Jesus. Rather the sick *were brought* by someone who cared about them. This happened for a variety of reasons, such as the person's physical weakness or immobility, a fear of being rejected, or disbelief in the possibility of being healed. Whatever the reason, the infirm were unable to come on their own and needed someone to assist them. Who brought them? People like you and me who know others who suffer from various ailments, especially cancer, depression, disability, and conditions associated with aging. How do we bring people to the divine Healer? We could be direct caregivers or we might be carrying them through our prayers, trusting that whatever form of healing they most seek will be given. Never doubt that praying for suffering people can make a difference. Their illness may or may not dissipate but they can receive courage, comfort, strength, peace, and other essential gifts of inner healing. When the ill ask you to pray, write down their names, hold these names close to your heart, and send forth God's love to them.

What suffering person will you bring to God through your prayer today?

Checking on My Motivations

Do everything for the glory of God.

1 Corinthians 10:31

Paul advocates doing everything for the glory of God. That's a tall order. "Everything" includes all thoughts, words, and deeds from the time of awakening in the morning until the last yawn before falling asleep at night. I wonder if we can ever have a completely pure motivation for anything, let alone *everything*. Paul recognizes this challenge. He uses the word "try: "just as I *try* to please everyone in every way, not seeking my own benefit..." (1 Corinthians 10:33). It is impossible to please everyone, just as it is highly improbable to avoid seeking a bit of our own benefit in much of what we do. Still, doing all for the glory of God remains the appropriate goal. I know how quickly I can slip into ego-motivation and self-absorption. I decided some time ago to begin each day with the following prayer as I wake up: I touch my forehead, mouth, heart, and hands as I say, "May all I think, speak, feel, and do be for your honor and done with love." This helps to keep me on the right track and leads me back when I fall off of it.

How would you describe the central motivation for what you do throughout the day?

Choosing to Be Positive

When ridiculed, we bless; when persecuted, we endure; when slandered, we respond gently.

1 Corinthians 4:12–13

Eckhart Tolle's book *The Power of Now* revitalized my desire to live the Christian message as expressed in 1 Corinthians 4:12–13. Tolle suggests that whenever we are about to judge someone harshly, when we want to respond with a negative remark or angry gesture, we pause and replace the negative with a positive. This reversal of desire takes considerable determination and practice. In busy traffic, I want to repay one discourtesy with another. When spoken to harshly, I want to bite back verbally. When treated with disrespect, I want to do something just as nasty in return. That is the natural, human inclination due to the way a part of the human brain works. This does not, however, make it right to respond in this way, and this is not the approach Jesus taught. He urged the opposite response: to counter negativity with kindness. Destructive thinking and acting beget more spitefulness. Constructive thinking and acting encourage a constructive response. Fortunately, we have another part of our brain that can choose to respond positively. The grace of God can help us do so.

What would help you to regularly replace a negative with a positive?

Christian Duties

They are to slander no one, to be peaceable, considerate, exercising all graciousness toward everyone.

Titus 3:2

In Paul's letter to Titus, he reminds us of what it means to be a Christian. While Paul lists some of the duties for the early Christians living on the island of Crete, these enduring and essential obligations apply equally to those of us now. If we could embody these responsibilities that reflect the teachings of Jesus, what a difference it would make—not only in our personal life but in the life of others, as well. We might begin by trying to act on one of the suggested duties each day. On Sunday we would do our best to avoid speaking unkindly toward anyone. On Monday we would make an effort to be as genuinely peacefully as possible, avoiding arguments and letting go of the need to be proven right. On Tuesday we would meet the challenge of being considerate to *everyone* (no exceptions). On Wednesday we would make every attempt to be a gracious presence no matter what happened. And then we would start over again, living these duties each day for the rest of the week. Now, if we did this, what a spirit-transforming week it could be.

Which of the duties that Paul mentions do you most put into practice?

Close to God's Heart

After [Jesus] placed his hands on them, he went away.

Matthew 19:15

Countless paintings depict a familiar gospel scene: children being brought to Jesus that he might "lay his hands on them and pray" (Matthew 19:13). Artists may well find themselves drawn to portray this particular moment in Jesus' life because of the tenderness this story evokes. Imagine the joy that blessing these children instilled in Jesus. Here he is in his public ministry, offering teachings that lead some people to treat him as an enemy, teachings that even his own disciples do not always understand or accept. As Jesus pauses in the midst of this ministry, which surely must have included some discouragement and loneliness, the children come to him with their wide eyes, contagious enthusiasm, ready smiles, and eager acceptance. They gather around Jesus in trust, sensing the kindliness flowing from him. In turn, the children's laughter and enjoyment brings Jesus the possibility of restoring his depleted energy and easing his sore spirit. Let us remember how close children are to the heart of God. Whether as a parent, teacher, daycare worker, relative, pastor, neighbor, or friend, we can bless children with our respect, kindness, joy, and prayer.

What response does the scene of Jesus blessing children call forth in you?

Come Away and Rest Awhile

> "Come away
> by yourselves
> to a deserted
> place and
> rest a while."
>
> *Mark 6:31*

Henri Nouwen wisely noted: "Somewhere we know that without a lonely place our lives are in danger." Jesus and Nouwen were not referring to loneliness. They were urging a temporary departure from others in order to have essential space for a healthy inner life. Jesus' invitation came from his immersion in constant activity. People hungered for his presence and healing abilities. He knew the value of going apart for prayer and renewal. Every person needs some solitude. "Going apart" does not mean being alone to catch up on social media. Rather, solitude involves a deliberate pause, letting go for a while of whatever grabs our attention. Parents with young children long to have even snippets of this space. So do people forced to work two or three jobs to pay bills. Monks and nuns would seem to have a sufficient amount of solitude, but even they must often make real efforts to attain enough quiet time due to their communal schedule. Rather than bemoaning the inhumane tendency of people's being busy every moment of their waking hours, it is more valuable to set an example by tending to our own necessary solitude.

Where and when do you experience solitude?

Come to Me

"Come to me, all you who labor and are burdened and I will give you rest."

Matthew 11:28

Who among us does not know the feeling of being burdened? Whether those heavy loads result from our own or from another's experience, the invitation Jesus extends in Matthew's gospel provides significant reassurance for us. We are not promised that our burdens will be immediately lifted but that we will be given "rest." Heartache may remain, physical and emotional pain persist, troubling concerns linger, and financial deficits continue. In the midst of what is not quickly changed or lessened, Jesus offers the gift of abiding peace. The word "come" tells us a lot. It contains both invitation and reception. It speaks of approaching and being assured of a welcome. Both comfort and strength of helpful proportion wait to infuse our spirit if we ease ourselves into the divine embrace, if we let go of our tight hold on how we insist life ought to be. Jesus invites us, "I am with you. Come, draw near. Sit beside me. Lean your head on my shoulder. You don't have to do or say anything. Let my love slip inside your heart. I will give you rest."

What part of your life is burdened and could benefit from the rest that Jesus offers?

Compassion, Come Quickly

May your compassion quickly come to us, for we are brought very low.

Psalm 79:8

As I look back in memory at the different circumstances that brought me "very low," I swiftly recall the people whom I believe were motivated by God to ease my distress. Each person offered nonjudgmental understanding and a patient, listening ear. They never gave up on me, no matter how much I repeated my woes or expressed my grief. Each extended a tender recognition of the suffering that pressed upon me. I felt their empathy. When they compassionately acknowledged my hurt they gathered me to their heart in a supportive kinship. This communion enabled me to find the necessary strength to face what could not be avoided. As I remember these supportive persons, I realize anew that the Holy One's compassion moves in our lives and slowly heals us through human beings. Choosing to be there for others when they suffer takes considerable, caring effort. We do not always feel like entering into another's pain. If compassion is to *come quickly*, we will need to step aside from our own desires and duties in order to enter into the lives of those bent low from suffering.

How have you experienced compassion, either for yourself or for another?

Constant Hope

Constant has been my hope in you.

Psalm 71:6

A friend of mine confided about the current situation with her elderly parents after she spent several overnights at their apartment. Her almost-blind father was incapable of taking care of her mother, who had unexpected health issues requiring minor surgery. My friend did not complain as she described never knowing when she would be called to be there for her father and mother. She did not whine when she indicated her inability to make definite plans for much of anything due to the need to be constantly available. In drawing our conversation to a close, she said, "When I get to the end of my rope, I find it always grows a little longer." What a positive attitude. That's hope, constant hope, grounded in a superb faith in God. My friend has an unwavering trust. She believes firmly that her ever-present Companion will provide strength and patience when she's most in need of it. In distressing times like hers, let us turn to Eternal Hope and be reminded of the first part of the verse in Psalm 71:6: "On you I depend from birth; from my mother's womb you are my strength."

On a scale from 1 to 10, how would you evaluate your "constant hope"?

Dark Valleys

Even though I walk in the dark valley, I fear no evil.

Psalm 23:4

For over thirty-five years I have companioned dedicated laypeople coming for spiritual guidance. They entrust to me the joys and sorrows of their lives in order for us to search within these events for where God is present and for how they might grow from these experiences. Few of us escape the "dark valleys" of Psalm 23. Some of us encounter these gloomy periods often, perhaps even daily. They come in the form of mental illness, unexpected tragedy, struggles with addiction, chronic illness, persistent anxiety, discouragement, sorrow, depression, many forms of loss, physical debilitation, and numerous other experiences of vanished joy and stifled hope. Psalm 23 was written thousands of years ago to assure each one in their dark-valley times that they are cared for unceasingly by the Good Shepherd. Even though we may be unaware of this presence, the psalmist assures us that our Compassionate Companion never abandons us. Instead, we will be given what we need to make it through our dark valley: repose, refreshment, guidance, courage, nourishment, goodness, and kindness. Read the psalm aloud, slowly. Let each line greet you with a rekindling of hope.

When have you most needed the message of Psalm 23?

Day and Night Impart Knowledge

Day pours out the word to day, and night to night imparts knowledge.

Psalm 19:3

What word does day pour out? What knowledge does night impart? If I observe life closely, each turning of day or night holds the possibility of discovering another facet of the Holy One for my faith life. The psalms often use creation as a source of learning more about the qualities of God. Taking out the sack of garbage on a cold winter's night, I am astounded by the stars' brilliance and recognize my smallness within the immensity of the cosmos. When an early morning sunrise startles me with its richness of color, my heart turns easily toward hope and gratitude for the gracious gift of a new day of life. Many times I have experienced how the natural world draws me inward to make a connection with the Creator. It teaches me: "You are not alone. You are part of a vast universe held in the Holy One's embrace. This natural world that stuns you with its beauty and vastness is but a small reflection of the Holy One's essence." If I remain open and aware, I can constantly be drawn closer to the Author of Life.

What aspect of nature most draws you to the Creator?

Excuses, Excuses

> Say not,
> "I am too
> young."
> To whomever
> I send you,
> you shall go.
>
> *Jeremiah 1:7*

Excuses, excuses. I've had my share of them, as you have probably had. (Too inexperienced, too old, too shy, too overly scheduled, too uneducated, too this, and too that.) "I'll go visit that person in the Care Center when my workload lessens." "I'll send a message of comfort after I find the right card." "I'll volunteer to be a catechist when I know more about my faith." "I'll help out at the food pantry once I get more comfortable with those who use it." "I'll speak to her after she apologizes." On and on the excuses go, and all the while the Holy One urges us to forgo those reasons and share the love planted in our hearts. Jeremiah dragged his feet but finally relented and did say "yes" to God. It is all right to voice excuses. This gives us an opportunity to sort out what causes our resistance and to gain clarity regarding our motivation. But eventually we have to put those excuses behind us and go, just as Jeremiah did, trusting in the Holy One's grace to assist us in doing what is ours to do.

What excuses do you use for withholding your "yes" to God?

False Motivation

"Take care not to perform religious deeds in order that people may see them."

Matthew 6:1

One Sunday at the Eucharistic liturgy I was sitting in a position where the celebrant could clearly see me. When it came time for taking up the offertory collection I began to squirm inside of myself. I had already given a donation to a food pantry earlier that week, which was all my limited budget would allow. But out of fear that I might be judged as "a stingy old nun," I opened up my billfold and added to the collection basket when it came by. Ever done something like that—doing something that appears worthy but really doing it for the wrong reason? False motivation, indeed. My action came from an ego-orientation. I wanted to "look good," to be thought well of, to be seen as contributing and acting justly. These are not "bad" desires unless they are attached to a false motivation like mine was. When we do something to benefit ourselves by gaining the approval of others, rather than responding because it's the appropriate or right thing to do, we're walking in the footsteps of those folks that Jesus chastised. Now, that's definitely not a pleasant thought.

Is there a motivation in some part of your life that requires changing?

Forgive Others Their Trespasses

> "If you forgive others their transgressions, your heavenly Father will forgive you."
>
> *Matthew 6:14*

Forgiveness has to be one of the most difficult spiritual practices. I have met only a few persons who seem to forgive easily. Most, including myself, hang onto old hurts until they become like a pile of dirty laundry. The clothes won't be clean unless we do something about them. It takes effort and time to put clothes in the washing machine, add soap, take the clothes out, and then dry and fold them. The same with forgiving others. Forgiveness does not happen without deliberate effort on our part. No wonder Jesus placed this as part of his prayer. We will not forgive fully without bringing our hurts and resentments to the One with the power to heal through us. Forgiveness is not something we do entirely on our own. We must pray to have the courage and humility to forgive another. Rabbi Rami Shapiro writes that "forgiveness is not forgetting, excusing, accepting, denying, or numbing" ourselves to pain. "Forgiveness is letting go." Prayer readies our heart and mind to finally let go of what diminishes our love and squashes our kindness to the size of a pebble.

What efforts best assist you when you need to forgive someone?

Getting into the Boat

They themselves got into boats and came to Capernaum looking for Jesus.

John 6:24

I marvel at the people's determined effort to find Jesus after he moved on from them. They expended considerable energy in looking for the Teacher who inspired and filled them with hope. His kindling of their minds and hearts stimulated this resolve to find him, and it appears they were not going to give up doing so. When I was a novice in my religious community, I learned to meditate and readily took time for this, along with reflecting on the Scriptures and extending kindness toward my community members, seeing qualities of Jesus in them. As I grew older and became absorbed in my ministry, some of that passion lessened. There are days now when I do not feel like praying, when I find all sorts of excuses to forgo morning meditation. There are situations when the last thing I want to do is find a Christlike quality in an irksome person. There are moments when I prefer being anything but my best self. That's when "the boat" arrives and I get into it, when I go beyond my apathy or negativity and set out "looking for Jesus."

How would you describe the quality or intensity of your relationship with God?

God Speaks

From the pillar of cloud he spoke to them.

Psalm 99:7

Verse seven from Psalm 99 refers to God speaking to Moses and his people. This communication happened quite frequently as they made their way through the wilderness in their long exodus to the Promised Land. We often read in various Biblical passages how God speaks to individuals, but what does it mean to "hear God speaking"? I have never heard a clear voice, yet I often sense the Holy One giving me guidance and confirmation of what to do and how to grow. Most recently, when I felt deluged in office details, I turned to Rabindranath Tagore's poetry after my meditation. I opened randomly to "Grandfather's Holiday" in which the poet describes working in his study and being interrupted by an active grandchild. God woke me up with the line "trapped in my work like a spider-webbed fly." Upon reading the poem's last line where Tagore addresses his grandchild, "You're the one who teaches me to let myself go," the Holy Spirit "told" me to lighten up, to not let my work hold me captive like a spider in a web. This is how God speaks to me.

How does God "speak" to you?

God's Decrees

Your decrees are...the joy of my heart.

Psalm 119:111

I wish I could always say God's decrees are the "joy of my heart." I have a ways to go on that one, especially when they require eliminating my desire for a neatly scheduled day and plenty of time for self-satisfying projects. Decrees such as "go the extra mile, give and not count the cost, welcome the stranger, visit the sick and imprisoned" do not exactly delight my heart when I'm struggling with meeting deadlines of my own making. However, once I let go of my cherished wants and follow through with action for others I *do* have joy in my heart. When I give of my carefully guarded time or limited finances to someone in need, I know it is the right thing to do. There is satisfaction in this reality. That is when God's decrees resemble joy rather than unwanted demands. Psalm 119 also notes that God's decrees "are my counselors" (v. 24). These dictates can guide us to live as our best self and nudge us to be persons of generous love, the kind that is reflective of Jesus, our superb teacher.

When have God's decrees been a source of gladness for you?

Guide Me, Teach Me

Guide me in your truth and teach me.

Psalm 25:5

Many a day I have paused in my work to ask for divine guidance. I look for this inner direction in a variety of situations. Sometimes I feel disgruntled regarding someone who neglected to meet my expectations of what I hoped they would have taken care of, such as providing detailed information for a retreat program. When this is the case, I ask my Inner Guide to show me how to change my attitude, to know what I can do to turn the corner of my irritation or discouragement and move toward something positive. At other times, I ask for guidance in my writing, when words or ideas remain hidden from me and I am blank in thought or scrambling around on the keyboard trying to put something together that has meaning and inspiration. I seek guidance regarding my daily schedule, for making choices about who I can assist and how to do this, and for not taking on too much. The content is endless regarding my need of God's guidance. I'll never stop seeking this assistance, and I'll never stop being grateful for it.

For what in particular do you seek God's guidance?

Here I Am

"Here I am"
he answered.

Genesis 46:2

God calls Jacob "in a vision by night." After Jacob answers, "Here I am," the Holy One encourages him go forth and not be afraid. This pattern repeats itself with other biblical personages. Most often the visit comes when one is caught off guard. They hear their name called. When they respond with "Here I am," they are encouraged to let go of hesitation and fear. Eventually, each person replies positively to the invitation extended to him or her, even if it is not something they want to do. Each reply of "Here I am" indicates a willingness to listen and accept the Holy One's message. Mary of Nazareth's response, "May it be done to me according to your word" clearly indicates what "Here I am" implies—a complete availability to God. We can find this biblical pattern in our lives too. The call often comes in uncertain, stressful times when we feel most vulnerable. We gradually sense what the Holy One requests. Then, we speak our "Here I am" with openness, confident that we, too, can alter our life accordingly, even if we prefer not to do it.

When have you responded "Here I am" to God, even though you preferred not to do so?

Hidden Things of the Heart

> "Although you have hidden these things from the wise and the learned you have revealed them to the childlike."
>
> *Matthew 11:25*

The "wise and the learned" carry knowledge within them that children do not have, due to their lack of lived experience or their undeveloped ability to express themselves. While the gift of knowledge provides valued benefits, it also contains the potential of keeping the mind blocked from receiving what the spirit needs for growth. Too much emphasis on mental intelligence tends toward an imbalanced self-importance and the unwillingness to listen and learn from what is observed. No wonder Jesus refers to children as the ones who discover the hidden things of the heart. I have watched children with their parents in supermarkets. The parent is intent on one thing only, securing what is on the shopping list. In the meantime, the child reaches out to touch colors on packages, picks up fruit and smells it, and pokes around longingly in the candy rack. In our faith life, we might consider being more like a child in a supermarket, exploring and examining what we believe, peeking inside the treasures of spirituality that we pass by in our hurry to be productive. Let us uncover the hidden things in our hearts.

How do you uncover the hidden things in your heart?

Honest Prayer

My prayer has been prompted by my deep sorrow and misery.

1 Samuel 1:16

In the story of Hannah we learn that she "remained long at prayer" because of her distraught condition of being childless (1 Samuel 1:12). She expresses her unhappiness as she pours out her anguish and distress to God. She then departs her prayer time with a sense of peace, having released her pain into the hands of the Compassionate One, whom she believes will hold it with care. Eventually, Hannah does conceive a child, the prophet Samuel. Hannah's experience of declaring her distress when she prayed does not imply that everyone's cries to God will necessarily be answered as directly as hers. Rather, it confirms the possible serenity that follows honest prayer like Hannah's. She held nothing back in approaching God with her distress. She was not afraid to describe how she felt. Peace settled inside of her after she cried out. (She "no longer appeared downcast" [v. 18].) This emotional and mental change came about because Hannah chose to be truthful and open with God about how she felt. She believed God would accept her honesty for what it was and that all would be well, no matter what happened.

What thoughts and feelings do you honestly bring to God today?

In Need of Divine Assistance

I will thrust you from your office and pull you down from your station.

Isaiah 22:19

Isaiah places these harsh words in the mouth of God to warn the people of their egotism and immorality. They acted as if they were totally in charge of their lives, had no need of divine assistance, and could do anything they desired. They had forgotten that God was the originator of their lives and of their ability to be prosperous. They became arrogant in assuming total self-sufficiency and presumed wrongly that they had no need of divine support. With this attitude, they then believed they could do what they pleased, regardless of the consequences of how this behavior affected others. When I reflect upon this message for my own life, I am called to consider whether or not I turn sufficiently toward the Holy One for support and guidance. How much do I go about my life as if it was all up to me? And do I consider how my thoughts and actions affect others? Anytime I think myself beyond the need of divine grace, I know my life to be headed toward spiritual disaster, just as the people of Isaiah's day moved toward their misfortune.

How much do you count on divine assistance?

Judging Others

Let the one among you who is without sin be the first to throw a stone at her.

John 8:7

Imagine what must have arisen in the minds of those ready to throw stones. Here they are, smugly sure of someone else's sin, until Jesus challenges them to recall their own wrongdoings. Surely they recalled memories of their own transgressions. How quickly we humans block out our own misdeeds and false actions and leap hungrily to condemn another person's. Negative judgment of others swiftly moves into self-righteousness and feelings of superiority. If we could sit next to someone and peer into his or her mind and heart for a day, we might well find numerous reasons to extend compassion for their behavior, rather than stinging accusations. None of us truly knows the full story of another. So often what we think about others or believe about them is off the mark. Monk and mystic Wayne Teasdale writes, "We can only judge others if we can fulfill two conditions: that we know the other's heart totally, and that we love them unconditionally. Only God can possibly meet these two conditions, therefore only God can judge. Despite this truth, people continue to play God, and pass on harsh and unfair judgments."

What has it been like for you to be in a situation where you were judged unfairly?

Laws That Guide Us

I will put my laws in their hearts.

Hebrews 10:16

This verse from Hebrews expresses the basic truth that God's law is written in our hearts, the inner space referring to our hidden self—such as thought, emotion, and intuition. I have never been fond of "laws." My independent nature fights the idea of too many rules and restrictions, especially overly rigid ones that confine my innate freedom to choose and act. Still, I know certain regulations to be absolutely necessary. We cannot have a peaceful, caring society without them. I know, too, that we are unable to live a moral life without foundational laws to guide us, such as the Ten Commandments. Balance is needed between inner and outer regulations. Personal prayer keeps us in touch with God's fundamental law of love residing in us. Because we are not always in touch with our inner self, the external laws of society and church serve to keep us headed in the right direction. These laws bring us back to center when our moral life starts to fall apart due to poor choices and decisions. If God's law is written in our hearts, then we had better peek in there regularly.

How do you respond to laws that are meant to guide you?

Let Go and Trust

He shouted, "Jesus, Son of David, have pity on me!"
Luke 18:38

A blind man sits at the roadside begging, something he has done ever since losing his sight. As a noisy crowd approaches, he senses their excitement and wants to know what is happening. The people refuse to answer his question. Instead, they scold and tell him to shut up because his cries create a distraction from what they are experiencing. But the man refuses to accept their rebuke and keeps on shouting, "Hey, I'm over here. I need your help." This is one determined man, not about to give up. Eventually, Jesus not only hears the man's plea but goes over to him and heals his blindness. What a lesson we can learn from this person who was desperate in his pleading and would not give up until he was heard. I admire his unswerving focus and I ask myself, "Am I that vulnerable and persistent in my prayer? Am I humble enough to cry out unswervingly, 'Have compassion on my struggles. Pay attention to what causes me suffering'?" To do so means I keep crying out with faith, believing the divine Healer will hear and draw near.

How would you answer the questions in this reflection?

Mercy and Compassion

> "Go and learn
> the meaning of
> the words,
> 'I desire mercy,
> not sacrifice.'"
>
> *Matthew 9:13*

When Pope Francis declared "A Year of Mercy," I pondered what "mercy" meant. I felt a bit confused because many consider this virtue to be interchangeable with compassion. Actually, the two entail different motivations and actions. Compassion involves an awareness of suffering with the intention of alleviating it. Mercy requires an intention to forgive someone who caused wrongdoing. These two virtues live side by side. How do we offer compassion to someone who is suffering if that someone seriously hurt us? We cannot do so without being merciful. Compassion can only happen if we have a mind and heart willing to forgive and not seek revenge. Unless we are merciful we will have a difficult time trying to be compassionate toward certain people who suffer, such as a divisive family member who develops an incurable disease, or a devious colleague whose lies punctured our relationship and now seeks support after her husband's betrayal, or a friend who damaged our family's reputation and now grieves the suicide of her son. Both mercy and compassion need a home in us. Let us continue to strengthen both of these essential virtues.

Which virtue, compassion or mercy, has the truest home in you?

Motes of Kindness

For steadfast is his kindness toward us.
Psalm 117:2

Even when life appears most troublesome, I can usually discover kindness somewhere. I've learned that this detection takes prayerful practice and the cultivation of a keen awareness each day. Otherwise, I miss what's around me because of the seeming insignificance of things. To help with being able to notice something encouraging, I've developed an evening prayer that includes looking back over the day for a piece of kindheartedness or beauty that slipped in between the activities. If I listed these "findings" they would include such things as the look of contentment on a stranger's face, being welcomed by an eager puppy at a friend's door, a green traffic light that kept me from being late, the first flower after a long winter, words of affirmation in an email, the sound of happy wrens in an evergreen tree. These are not big, showy items. That is the wonder of divine love. All sorts of unnoticed motes of kindness float our way, but in the rush of life they glide right past our non-awareness. Perhaps if you look tonight you will find a kindness hidden within your day.

When has awareness of a small kindness or a piece of beauty buoyed your spirit?

No Going Back to Normal

He came home.

Mark 3:20

How would it feel to be away from the home where you grew up, to return to where you enjoyed family and friends and felt a closeness to them, and hear them say: "You are out of your mind!"? What a blow to good memories and a sense of belonging. How crushing to one's self worth. Those words must have seared the happiness in Jesus' heart. When he returned home he was definitely not the "same old Jesus" who had grown up there. He arrived as a revered teacher with a significant following. This disrupted their normal routine and notions of him. ("The crowd gathered, making it impossible for them even to eat" [Mark 3:20].) Those who had known Jesus could not figure out why he had such a following. The change they saw in him shook apart their assumptions of who he was during his years of living near them. So they tried to rid themselves of him, to get things "back to normal" by chasing him out. But there was no going back to normal. The same for us once our heart comes to value the love and goodness of Jesus.

How do you respond when someone you care about reveals changed behavior?

Offering Mercy

Should a man refuse mercy to his fellows, yet seek pardon for his own sins?

Sirach 28:4

Years ago I experienced a hurtful betrayal by a member of my community who was in leadership. Decades later when she neared her final years I found myself in a situation where I could have treated her in a belittling way. I am grateful for the grace to have risen above that possibility and turned toward her, instead, with compassion for her mental vulnerability and physical diminishment. The author of the Book of Sirach makes it clear that we cannot expect forgiveness and mercy unless we also extend these virtues to others who make life difficult for us. Jesus, too, stressed how indispensable these core elements were to his teachings. How can it be, then, that those who claim to be devoted Christians are parents disowning their children, siblings refusing to speak to each other, adherents of religious communities holding grudges and deliberately avoiding reconciliation, church leaders and members clinging to alienation and hostility? What leads these committed Christians to ignore or dismiss the most basic requirements of their religion? Let us pray that our own hearts express mercy toward anyone who brings hurt into our lives.

When have you had the opportunity to offer mercy to someone who offended you?

Offering Our First Fruits

Bring a sheaf of the first fruits of your harvest.

Leviticus 23:10

The season of summer, laden with an abundance of fruits and vegetables, provides an excellent metaphor to reflect on the plenitude of our inner realm. In doing so, Leviticus does not simply indicate that we bring some fruits of our spiritual harvest, but the *first* fruits. What might these be? "First fruits" indicates the best of the season, the least blemished, the most delicious. (If you have ever had a garden or orchard you know what Leviticus means. The first meal of asparagus, the best ripened peach: oh, how we enjoy the fresh, vivid tastes.) What, then, we are to bring to God? Certainly this includes the finest of our prayer life. If we wait until the end of the day for a quiet time to reflect, we may well bring more sleepy weariness than bright attentiveness. If we start the day by offering the first fruits of our prayer, we come with a freshness of mind, body, and spirit. We can more easily be present and alert. This "first fruit" allows us to enter into prayer with a greater readiness to respond to the stirrings of the Spirit.

How would you describe the first fruits that you offer to God?

One Loaf Makes a Difference

"Give it to the people to eat," Elisha said.

2 Kings 4:42

This account from the Second Book of Kings correlates to the gospel accounts that describe a few loaves of bread feeding a hungry crowd. In both situations those who have a small amount disbelieve the possibility that so many people could be fed with so little. They express amazement when the people's hunger is satisfied with what initially seemed to be extremely sparse. In our troubled world today we might also feel that our "few loaves"—our small efforts—can do little to ease the amount of suffering that exists. But what if our individual gestures of compassion, our personal prayer, our lone voice speaking for justice, were joined by thousands of others? What a difference that could make. I recall Amnesty International sending a message from a political prisoner who was freed. She said, "It was the hundreds of postcards people sent telling me to not give up that kept my hope alive." Similarly, I have heard desperately ill people say that knowing people were praying for them gave them strength to endure their pain. Never doubt that our "one loaf" can make a big difference.

What "one loaf" will you supply for someone today?

Pouring Out

For I am already being poured out like a libation.

2 Timothy 4:6

Being poured out, being emptied—this recurring message resounds in Paul's letters to the early Christians. This is not surprising. Paul was inspired by Jesus, who gave completely of himself. ("He [Jesus] emptied himself..." [Philemon 2:7].) No wonder Paul urges the followers of Jesus to do the same. Yet what a challenging teaching. Who wants to be poured out? Not me. I much prefer being filled to the brim. Yet I know I am not meant to hoard what I receive, whether this consists of something material or spiritual. The kindness someone offers me, I am to share. The time and attention I receive when I am hurting, I am to extend to another in need. The pardon easing my wounded self, I am to release for the one asking my forgiveness. Long ago, my novice directress emphasized, "You cannot give what you do not have." Thus, it is essential to try daily to restore and refill my emptied self through spending time with God in prayer. That way I have something to give when the time comes to be "poured out like a libation."

How are you being asked to pour out your gifts for others?

Practice What You Preach

For they preach but they do not practice.

Matthew 23:3

Jesus chided teachers of religious law for their duplicity, but his comment applies to anyone claiming to be a Christian but who does not apply the gospel teachings to how they behave. I thought of this when I boarded a plane for home. I heard a young woman ask the man next to her if he would exchange his aisle seat for her middle one. She explained how she gets panic attacks and feels safest next to the aisle. The man refused. I sat one row ahead in my aisle seat. I hesitated. I thought about the four-hour flight in that tight middle seat. Then I recalled what I teach in the Boundless Compassion programs: to have empathy for others by imagining what it is like for them to experience what they do. I stood up and offered the frightened woman my place. The relief in her "thank you" told me I made the appropriate choice. My action contained a slight gesture of kindness but I knew if I did not "walk my talk" in that little way, I would not manage to do so when a more challenging situation came along.

Who has helped you to practice what you preach?

Pray Always

He told them a parable about the necessity for them to pray always without becoming weary.

Luke 18:1

There are two noteworthy phrases in this verse from Luke's gospel: *pray always*, and *without becoming weary*. Prayer consists foremost of an intention of the heart: I *intend* to be in union with God. I focus my desire on enjoying and growing more loving through this relationship. To pray *always* does not imply that I am continually uttering words in order to experience this union. Rather, *always* means that I persistently desire to have God in my heart. I intend to keep this inward goal alive wherever I am. My mind may be occupied with constant obligations but my heart leans toward this inner union. *Without becoming weary* implies that I do not give up on my yearning to stay closely united with my Beloved Companion even when the distance between us might seem vast, or when the distraction of duties impinges upon it. In meditation and other forms of prayer, I do not tire of turning my attention again and again toward this communion, trusting that the Holy One knows the desires of my heart and loves me no matter how distracted or preoccupied I might be.

What choices and decisions enable you to "pray always without becoming weary"?

Praying in Desolate Times

Many say, "Oh, that we might see better times!" O Lord, let the light of your countenance shine upon us!

Psalm 4:7

How readily any of us in this current era of turmoil could exclaim, "Oh, that we might see better times!" The extensive alienation in both global and national spheres can quickly lead us to feel engulfed in the implied darkness of Psalm 4:7. Fortunately, the psalmist does not stop by simply bemoaning how terrible things are. In the next breath, a spirit of hope rises within the prayer. The psalmist asks, not only for God's light to shine upon the people, but that this radiance emit from a divine "countenance." This request implies an intimacy, the very face or closeness of divinity. It suggests an underlying belief that the Holy One, who is Eternal Light, can and will assist humanity's longing for a world where justice and peace bring about harmony and well-being, especially for those caught in the trap of inequality and poverty. Hard times need not be the end of the story. We have a divine presence whose radiance comes close to us, showing us the way out of the bleakness. Let us embrace that light and allow the divine radiance to show in our speech and actions.

How do you respond spiritually during difficult times?

Reconciling with Others

> **You are destined... to turn back the hearts of parents toward their children.**
>
> *Sirach 48:10*

Is there any one of us who does not know someone who has separated themselves from a parent, or a parent who has broken off ties with a child? Unfortunately, this alienation is an all too common experience. Even in the time of the prophet Elijah, this situation existed among families. A few years ago, I witnessed the power of love to bring about a much needed reconciliation. For years a man chose to never visit his father or communicate with him because this parent treated him poorly for much of his young life. Only after the adult son prayed to turn his heart around and chose to focus on finding the good in his father did he gradually forgive him. When he did so, both the father and son healed from their past hurts. Today that parent and child are close friends. To reconnect with anyone who has hurt us takes a lot of prayer, a big heart, and a large amount of vulnerability. We will never manage to reconcile with another unless we are willing to let go of the past and magnanimously open our heart to others in the way God does with us.

Is there anyone with whom you need to reconcile?

Responding Generously

The leprosy left him immediately.

Mark 1:42

Have you ever wondered how the healed leper might have gone on with his life after Jesus freed him from his appalling condition? When the man is healed of his devastating illness, Jesus tells him not to talk about it but the man does so anyway. In fact, the leper restored to health can't keep his mouth shut. He is immensely grateful, overwhelmed with joy to again be a part of society and to live without the disabilities and social stigma of his disease. But as the years went by, did he take the gift for granted? Did he eventually forget the Healer? Or did he give thanks each day for the rest of his life? Did he change in some significant way? Was the healed man more caring and understanding of others who were shunned? Was he extra generous with his presence and talents in helping those who were ill? I'd like to think so. I have not had leprosy, but God's grace has nurtured my growth in numerous ways. I am grateful. I want to show it by the way I live.

What healing grace has affected your life and how have you responded?

Returning from Exile

Then our mouth was filled with laughter, and our tongue with rejoicing.

Psalm 126:2

Psalm 126 refers to the Jewish people who were deported out of Jerusalem and sent to Babylon because of disputes among political leaders. These exiles did not return to their beloved homeland until decades later. No wonder they were filled with elation when they did finally set foot again in their own country. Psalm 126 describes their jubilation and full confidence that God will restore what has been destroyed. I come to this psalm recollecting my own and others' journeys, when we felt far from our inner homeland during situations such as a time of grief, nursing a sore relationship, healing from illness, or experiencing some form of inner discontent. At times like this, we can feel as though God is far from us, that we will never return to an inner homeland of peace and happiness. Psalm 126 assures us that God is with us; we will not remain exiled forever from our serenity. As we wait for a return from our state of despondency, the psalmist encourages us to keep our faith firmly planted in trust that God will bring us home to our joy.

Is there a part of your inner self that seems to be in exile?

Riches Lavished Upon Us

...the riches of his grace that he lavished upon us.

Ephesians 1:7–8

Two words, "riches" and "lavished," leap out of this passage from Ephesians, which refers to grace, the gift of an active, divine love flowing through every pore of what makes up our life. Those two words evoke a sense of abundance, unreserved treasure, and a copious outpouring of spiritual enrichment. What a contrast this divine generosity is in comparison to a human self-orientation that leans toward over-identification with scarcity—the fear of not having enough of what one possesses and values. This fear leads to a withholding of valuable time, attentive listening, compassionate concern, and other kindnesses. St. Paul assures us that in God's heart a plenitude of virtues awaits our reception—courage, patience, strength, confidence, refuge, openness, forgiveness, nonjudgment, generosity—whatever will aid us in living the day well in union with our Grace-Giver. All this is at our bidding if we turn toward this lavish Benefactor and open our inner being to receive what is offered. I often turn to a prayer of Julian of Norwich to help remember these riches of divine plenty: "God, of your goodness, give me yourself. For you are enough for me."

What would you name as some of the divine riches lavished upon you?

More Than Enough

The eyes of all look hopefully to you, and you give them their food in due season.

Psalm 145:15

In the Second Book of Kings, Elisha orders his servant to give the twenty loaves of bread to the people to eat. His servant protests, "There are a hundred people there. It's not enough." As it turns out, it is more than enough. In John's gospel, something similar occurs when Jesus asks Philip where they can buy sufficient bread for the crowd. Philip replies, "It would take two hundred days' worth of wages to feed that many." But the loaves again provide sufficient nourishment with some food left over. Before our investments took an enormous tumble, my community of ninety members was advised that our money would run out in less than ten years. Thankfully, we agreed to not give in to fear. We chose, instead, to focus on doing what we could to live simply and to have faith that, with God's help, our few loaves could multiply. As the years went by, we received unexpected monetary gifts due to the generosity of others. These helped us pay our debts. What a good lesson for us in how to trust when the cupboard looks empty.

How have you experienced the "multiplication of loaves" in your life?

Seeking and Finding

Such is the race...that seeks the face of the God of Jacob.

Psalm 24:6

Sometimes I wish I could stand up in church and ask the homilist for more information about his message. One of those situations happened recently when our pastor spoke about "looking for God." He encouraged those of us present to seek God everywhere and gave good examples of where to look: in shopping malls and crowded elevators, in supermarkets and busy offices, around family tables and in hospital rooms. I kept waiting to learn how we would know when we found this God we were to seek, but the homilist never gave any descriptions of this. So, how do we know? When we have a good feeling inside? When something unusual happens that connects us to an unseen presence? Perhaps. But I believe we mainly discover the presence of God when we experience anyone who reflects the attributes revealed in Jesus. We know we have come in touch with divinity when we meet such qualities as compassion, mercy, kindness, honesty, generosity, patience, understanding, nonjudgment, and forgiveness—all beautiful facets that shone forth from Jesus in his ministry and are reflected in others now, if we are ready to find them.

What facets of divinity have you recently noticed in those around you?

Seeking Wholeheartedly

Happy are they who observe [God's] decrees and seek [God] with all their heart.

Psalm 119:2

What does it mean to "seek God" and to do so with "all" of our heart? *Seeking* implies that we are putting some intention and energy into the process. We are making a deliberate effort. So many things try to pull us away from seeking spiritual growth with all our heart. Sometimes we do not even realize we are desiring material things with considerably more effort than we are the things of God. *Seeking* also suggests a belief that there is someone or something to be found at the end of the search. The dictionary offers the word "pursue" in place of "seek." That word is defined as "follow, hunt, chase, trail, track." Can we put that kind of purpose and spiritual exertion into our longing to pursue and track the Holy One more completely? This determined vitality, it seems to me, is what it means to seek the Holy One with "ALL" our heart—to daily focus intently and to yearn wholeheartedly for an ever truer relationship with this Cherished One, who also seeks our attention and desires our committed love.

What does "seeking God with all your heart" mean to you?

Sent Forth

He summoned the Twelve and gave them power.

Luke 9:1

What must the Twelve have felt when Jesus summoned and "sent them to proclaim the kingdom of God and to heal the sick" (Luke 9:2)? Did their egos momentarily become puffed up with their power—until the reality of what they were to do became clear to them? Did they then feel inadequate or fearful? Did they hesitate and question whether they were fully prepared for what lay ahead? There is no indication of this. Rather, the summoning is followed immediately with "Then they set out..." (v. 6). So the Twelve must have trusted the power given to them, believing they would have what was needed for each situation. There have been times when I longed to have that kind of trust, especially when I sensed an interior summoning to do something new. I remember feeling inadequate at the first retreat I gave, when I was assigned my first patient as a hospice volunteer, and the first time I sat across from another person as his spiritual director. My fear and anxiousness eventually eased with the realization that God's power was there for me if I would allow this gift to be used.

How do you see the power of God at work in your life?

Sing Joyfully

**Come, let us
sing joyfully
to the Lord.**

Psalm 95:1

While we may not always be humming a tune
to the Holy One, there are numerous opportunities to "sing joyfully." We may not think of
these as "songs," yet when satisfaction, gratitude,
relief, and consolation enter our days almost
imperceptibly, we quietly unite with the Joy of
All Hearts: rising in the morning with gladness
to be alive; the relief at hearing about a friend's
successful surgery; the kinship of prayer at liturgy; the humorous quote on social media; the
sparkle in the eyes of a child; the momentary
peace that fills the heart. Each of these merits
a song of praise. I know my heart is turning
toward the Joyful One when I go for walks each
day and a chant or a familiar song starts circulat-
ing in my memory. This happens when I observe
such things as foxes at play, a meandering river, a
woodpecker looking for insects on a tree trunk,
or the sound of the wind washing waves on the
lake. Joy can sit inside of us, but unless we open
the door of our awareness we will keep that visitor silently tucked away.

*What brings you joy in the midst
of your day?*

Small Acts of Great Love

"A mustard seed…is the smallest of seeds on the earth. But once it is sown, it springs up and becomes the largest of plants."

Mark 4:31–32

Chan Khong, a fourteen-year-old girl in Vietnam, wanted to help poor, hungry children in the local slums. She began by going to her neighbors and asking them to each put aside just three handfuls of rice a day for the children. With this tiny beginning, she was able to develop a program of care that, seven years later, involved ten thousand people working in it. Chan Khong said, "Do not despise the small act. Every small act, if you do it deeply, profoundly, can touch the whole universe. Millions of small acts will build a wonderful world." Her wisdom offers valuable impetus, especially if we think our tiny efforts do not make a difference. Jesus told his followers something similar: the kingdom of God grows through "the smallest of seeds." Those seeds are little acts of great love. What in your life seems insignificant? Making breakfast for someone? Taking ten minutes to listen? Making a phone call? Changing a diaper? Opening a car door? One kind deed can make a big difference. Look for the little things. Do the little things. They can change our world.

Do you believe in the value of your small deeds?

Sowing Bountifully

> **Whoever sows sparingly will also reap sparingly, and whoever sows bountifully will also reap bountifully.**
>
> *2 Corinthians 9:6*

My mentors of sowing bountifully have taught me a lot. I learned from them to not hesitate to give fully. My great aunt Ida was exemplary in this regard. Until my late teens I did not know how little she had financially, that the delicious sugar cookies she always kept on hand for company were baked from government subsidies. Aunt Ida's cheerful hospitality blessed every visitor. She managed to meet her basic needs and always found something to share. The same was true of Father Tom, pastor of a financially impoverished congregation. He continually gave his own money to those in need, assuring those of us concerned about his lack of personal funds that "God would provide." And God always did. About the time Father Tom's bank account neared empty, unexpected donations replenished it. These mentors of sowing bountifully remind each of us that we ought not to withhold what could enrich the life of someone else. Jesus understood this and exemplified it by sharing abundantly of his love and healing abilities. When the notion of scarcity shoves us toward fear of not having enough, let us continue to give generously.

Who are your examples of sowing bountifully?

Spending Time with the One We Love

They were overwhelmed with grief.

Matthew 17:23

When the disciples gathered in Galilee, Jesus predicted his forthcoming passion by telling them he was going to be rejected and killed (Matthew 17:22). Matthew tells us they were overwhelmed with sorrow at hearing this announcement. In spite of their blunders and inability to grasp the full message of his teachings, the disciples had given their hearts to Jesus. Having been with him constantly, the disciples continually witnessed what a magnificent, kindhearted being he was. They loved Jesus greatly, so it would be expected that they could not bear the thought of his death, especially a violent one. I can imagine how the suggestion of his having to suffer brutally left them feeling hollow and bereft. I think about their intense affection for Jesus, and I long for my own love to have that quality. As with the disciples, the only way my love will grow and strengthen is by spending time with Jesus, doing so by returning repeatedly to the gospels to encounter his life and teachings. Within the context of what Jesus said and did, I can find myself being drawn to him with an ever increasing fondness.

What qualities of Jesus most attract you to him?

Spiritual Nourishment

"Get up and eat, else the journey will be too long for you."

1 Kings 19:7

Elijah, afraid for his life, went fleeing through the desert. There he reached a point of such exhaustion and hopelessness that he wanted to succumb to death. That is when the angel approached Elijah, "touched him and ordered him to get up and eat." If Elijah had not followed this wise advice, he would never have made it to his destination or been able to give the valuable service he was meant to accomplish. Do you notice how we take spiritual sustenance for granted when life flows along smoothly? But let serious disruptions and ill-timed intrusions invade our controlled life and that's another matter. Health problems, pressured schedules, financial struggles, catastrophes at home or work, these things arise and there we are, forging ahead as if all depended solely on our determination and decisions. We forget that we, too, are to "get up and eat." That is, in those very times of unsettledness and adversity, we are like Elijah. We need to pause and partake of spiritual strength, the kind that comes with turning in prayer to the Source of Life who provides encouragement and hope.

What similarity do you find between Elijah's need for nourishment and your own?

Stay Awake

> "Therefore, stay awake! For you do not know on which day your Lord will come."
>
> *Matthew 24:42*

We do not know the precise moment when death will come for us. We are to be prepared for this unexpected visitor, but I prefer to be vigilant for a different reason. I choose to be awake, to enjoy life rather than focus on fear of death's imminence. Some years ago I read Stephen Levine's book *A Year to Live*, in which he suggests spending a year as if it were our last. I decided to do this and learned a new approach to living. I discovered that if I stay awake to what happens in daily life, I need not worry about death's arrival. I can relish life and not fear my last breath. If I try to be conscious of how I am living and responding spiritually each day, this alertness provides countless opportunities for growing in virtue. Endless situations arise to welcome Christ in others and live his teachings. I receive continual reminders to live gratefully and find untold prospects for responding to God's grace. If I am awake to these matters, then I need not live with concern about the timing of my death.

How do you "stay awake"?

137

Steadfast Steps

My steps have been steadfast in your paths, my feet have not faltered.

Psalm 17:5

Recently I visited a woman who fell by missing a step when she was walking. This misstep caused two broken bones in her neck, a gash on her forehead, and a badly bruised arm. How quickly a slip of the foot can undo a healthy physical life. In a comparable manner, just as quickly a slip on our spiritual path can leave our relationship with the Holy One bruised or damaged. One verbal misstep of ours through caustic language or intentional putdowns can cause injury to another person's peace and self-image. A harsh remark can taint a valued relationship. A deliberate lie can erase a strongly held trust. A thoughtless, false accusation can seriously mar a reputation. When these slips happen we lose our steadfastness on God's path. One of the ways we remain upright and steady when we move physically is by paying attention to where we walk and what lies ahead on the path. The same is true of our inner life. When we are attentive to our mental and emotional state of being we are less likely to cause hurt by falling into verbal missteps.

When have you lost your spiritual balance by being inattentive?

Stewards of Hidden Treasures

*...stewards of
the mysteries
of God.*

1 Corinthians 4:1

A steward is a servant, an assistant, one who manages a household or a business. The work of a steward is to oversee or supervise what is not owned or possessed. There are vast secrets encompassing the hidden truths contained in life, death, and everything in between that influence our relationship with the Holy One. How do we steward these mysteries? With careful attentiveness and openness to what they can teach us, doing so, certainly, with humble trustworthiness and without arrogance or a self-defensive posture. It seems bold to be a steward of "the mysteries of God," to be entrusted with these sacred treasures of wisdom, and then act as if I have more right to them than anyone else does. When we pray, speak, offer counsel, or teach about any aspect of the divine mysteries we are wise to turn constantly to the Holy Spirit and ask for faith and guidance. I find this to be absolutely necessary whenever I give a retreat or companion someone in spiritual direction. I count on my listening and speaking to be led and guided by the Holy One.

*What treasures of God do you especially
guard in your heart?*

Strive for Peace

**Strive for peace
with everyone.**

Hebrews 12:14

Peace, with *everyone*? Is this possible in a troubled society like ours? How can this be achieved within families, workplaces, church congregations, and nations where constant disharmony and antipathy exist? Jealousies and rivalries, competition for who is best or has the most, arguments over whose ideas are worthy and whose are not, broken relationships, resentment and bitterness caused from past hurts, power struggles and quarrelsome arrogance—the list of reasons for a lack of peace grows larger every day. Yet, I believe it is conceivable to attain peace with *everyone*. Here are some guidelines: Do not hold grudges. Let go of what steals your joy. Maintain kindness toward those who display a negative attitude. Refuse to make an enemy of those who consider you their enemy. Reconcile, even when you know it was not *your* fault. Try to perceive the deeper reason for someone's hurtful behavior. Do not dwell on troubling memories. Remember that you cannot force anyone to change. Having peace with others does not mean that everything works out well, or that we accept damaging behavior, but that we refuse to add to conflict and dissension.

*How will you strive
for peace today?*

ORDINARY TIME

The Crux of Hypocrisy

> "I thank you that I am not like the rest of humanity."
>
> *Luke 18:11*

Here is the crux of hypocrisy: it is based on a denial of how I could be like another person, especially if that person looks or acts in a way that is unacceptable in my eyes. Yet, the potential for good or for ill resides within each of us. In *With Open Hands*, Henri Nouwen addresses this reality: "With compassion you can say, 'In the face of the oppressed I recognize my own face and in the hands of the oppressor I recognize my hands. Their flesh is my flesh; their blood is my blood.'" One of the graced moments of my life was when I admitted to myself that I felt hatred for another person. I never thought I could feel this way about anyone and was appalled to find that emotional response within myself. This humbled me and led me to see how more alike I am than different from other human beings. That graced recognition has helped tremendously in being less judgmental of others. I do not accept inappropriate or harmful conduct but I know I have within myself the same propensity for what is said or done.

How do you find yourself being like "the rest of humanity"?

141

The Fidelity of Divine Love

Then I bathed you with water, washed away your blood, and anointed you with oil.

Ezekiel 16:9

In chapter 16 of Ezekiel, God speaks to Jerusalem through symbols of water, blood, and oil to emphasize divine mercy extended to a city in spite of its unfaithfulness. This beautiful passage of devoted attention reflects the generosity and fidelity of God and calls us to generate those same qualities in our relationships. This is especially required when the other person or persons do not act as we wish. They may be short-tempered when we want them to be carefree, silent when we would like them to speak, talkative when we wish them to be quiet, self-centered when we need them to give their attention to others. Our human tendency when this sort of thing happens is to respond negatively toward those who do not do as we wish. Jesus noted well that it is much easier to love those who love us than it is to reach out to those who fail us. It is tempting to close our hearts to someone who does not meet our expectations and conditions. The person of true care and kindness continues to offer a spacious and kind welcome in spite of personal disappointment.

What helps you to go beyond disappointment in others and continue to welcome them?

The Discipline of Attentiveness

You hate discipline and cast my words behind you.

Psalm 50:17

In praying Psalm 50, I wondered what kind of failed discipline causes the Holy One's words to be "cast behind" me. What would lead me to disregard what God desires? It didn't take long to come up with a central answer: it is the discipline of being alert in order to listen to the inner voice of the Spirit calling me toward what is good. Ongoing discipline of mind and heart requires that I be attentive and aware of what I am thinking and feeling. In doing so, I can then recognize the choices before me that lead toward or away from motivating faith and spiritual growth. How quickly I become immersed in social media or captured by the daily requirements of ministry. This absorption causes me to become totally caught up in my life and tasks, so much so that I forget the discipline of inner listening. At other times, I am quite simply too lethargic or indifferent to be observant. Those are some of the situations when I readily cast behind me the words of loving guidance extended by the Spirit.

How have you experienced the discipline of attentiveness to inner guidance?

The Guidance of Holy Wisdom

**I pleaded,
and the spirit
of Wisdom
came to me.**

Wisdom 7:7

"Pleaded" connotes a huge amount of humility. It implies that the options for self-determination and an inability to manage the situation alone have run out. Who of us likes to get down on our bumbling knees and implore Holy Wisdom for guidance? *Pleading* hints of "surrender" and who wants to totally give one's self in trust to this invisible Counselor? Our inclination leans toward being in charge, figuring things out by ourselves. This part of self, "the ego," seeks to be chief and master, locking us in our small world of security and power. Moving beyond this strong determination of the ego in order to receive Holy Wisdom's guidance requires openness to that which may not always "make sense," dreams and intuitive inclinations that are not easily explained. The spirit of Wisdom comes, not to put our plans in place according to our wants and desires, but to guide us toward what most grows us into holiness. Are we ready to plead for this? Are we ready to hand over our self to Holy Wisdom with trust that the way will be made known?

*How ready are you to plead and acknowledge
your need for assistance?*

The Quality of Our Hearts

> "A good tree does not bear rotten fruit, nor does a rotten tree bear good fruit."
>
> *Luke 6:43*

Jesus often referred to the landscape around him to present some basic principles. In the teaching from Luke's gospel he uses clear contrasts to make a point about the quality of our hearts. First, he compares good fruit to rotten fruit. Then he adds weight to this by reminding the people they cannot "pick figs from thorn bushes." As if that is not enough, Jesus tosses in yet another image by saying they cannot "gather grapes from brambles." He obviously felt rather strongly about this teaching: *the quality of what we do externally comes forth from how we are internally.* What is in the heart makes a great deal of difference. Our intentions matter. There are days when I am a tree with bushels of fine fruit. On other days nary an edible piece can be found. What makes the difference between the two? My "tree" lacks good fruit when I lose sight of who reigns at the center of my life, when I forget love as my core inspiration by concentrating only on my self-oriented desires, or when I act in a way that disparages others' well-being.

How would you describe your basic quality of heart in what you do?

The Virtue of Gentleness

We were gentle among you, as a nursing mother cares for her children.

1 Thessalonians 2:7

Can a person be vibrantly alive and also be spiritually gentle? Yes. I know this to be possible because of someone I worked with long ago. Fr. Killian Mooney was one of the gentlest persons I ever met. This soft-spoken, Trinitarian priest ministered to impoverished people in the hill country of southeastern Kentucky. In my mid-twenties, I went there several summers to assist with religious education programs among the mining communities. Fr. Killian's way with the people taught me much about gentleness. This virtue does not mean being passive, wimpy, or submissive. Quite the contrary. Gentleness weaves strong threads of kindness into an unbreakable quilt of compassion. This calm-mannered priest cared deeply about his flock and protected them fiercely, just "as a nursing mother cares for her children." He was a man of conviction, filled with kindheartedness and fully dedicated to a ministry of justice. Father Killian's presence enabled me to see that a spirituality of gentleness comes out of a strong respect for others. This virtue fosters an attitude of non-judgment and a belief that each person is worthy of dignity and acceptance.

How has other people's gentleness affected your life?

The Wine of Hidden Blessings

Now there were six stone water jars there for Jewish ceremonial washings.

John 2:6

What we plan is sometimes far from what God has in mind. I think of this in relation to the wedding feast at Cana. Everyone gathered for a festive wedding. Those who planned the gala event filled six stone jars of water so the guests could follow the custom of washing their hands before the bread was blessed. What the planners never considered was that those six jars of water would become filled with delicious wine. That's how it often is in our lives too. We set out the stone jar of our day and intend to fill it with all types of things that make up our scheduled events. Then our plans slowly, or quickly, fall apart with interruptions, disruptions, and other uncontrolled events. My first response when this happens is to feel impatient or frustrated. But when I pause and remember I am not the ultimate planner, I can usually find the wine of blessing hidden in my foiled endeavors. God is full of surprises, so it is best to keep our mind and heart open to the unexpected ways this unpredictable divinity manifests in our lives.

When has God manifested unexpectedly in your life?

The Wisdom of Elders

Then Eli understood that the Lord was calling the youth.

1 Samuel 3:8

While we may be familiar with the Scripture passage describing young Samuel being called by God and his eventual response of "Here I am," we my not be aware of a valuable detail in the story. The passage from the First Book of Samuel reveals a crucial component of Samuel's experience. This young person most probably would not have identified the voice calling him as that of God's had it not been for his mentor, Eli, an elder whose "eyes had lately grown so weak he could not see" (1 Samuel 3:2). Eli's external blindness contrasts with his perceptive, inner seeing. When Samuel thinks Eli is calling him, his mentor tells the youth to go back to sleep. Finally, Eli realizes who wants to contact his apprentice. Samuel would have missed this calling had it not been for his aged mentor. Eli's ripened faith recognizes the voice of God in what the youth misinterprets. This aged man epitomizes the wisdom that God bestows on older people so they can see what lies beneath the surface of life. Let us give thanks for the wise elders in our families and faith communities.

Who are the elders in your life who have guided you along the way?

Trust Our Efforts to Bear Fruit

Blessed are you who are now weeping, for you will laugh.

Luke 6:21

When we are in the throes of severe loss, it is almost impossible to believe we will feel happy again. In times of intense grief the thought of being able to laugh and enjoy life seems inconceivable. And yet, the day comes when little sunbeams of joy slip in between the cracks of our broken heart. Ever so slowly, our enthusiasm comes back to life. In the same way, we may find it difficult to believe the Beatitudes of Jesus, to imagine that people in tough economic and social conditions will have something better than they now have. Jesus looked much further and deeper than we do. His vision was large and expansive. Jesus expressed hope because he knew that injustice can be alleviated. He trusted that the kingdom of love held the power to bring about change. Jesus longed to have us believe, too, that a world of peace is possible if we live with integrity and become loving in the ways he prescribed. He wanted us to trust that our efforts could eventually make a difference, be they ever so small and incremental.

How does the way you live contribute to hopeful change for our society?

Turn the Other Cheek

> "When someone strikes you on [your] right cheek, turn the other one to him as well."
>
> *Matthew 5:39*

Jesus was an effective teacher. He could get across an important point in a variety of ways, one of which was by using hyperbole in his examples. In chapter five of Matthew's gospel, Jesus overstates what to do when confronted by violence. By saying, "Turn the other cheek," he emphasizes responding in a nonviolent manner when being attacked. This teaching is difficult to accept because our instinctual nature is to fight back, to have revenge, to show who is strongest, to be out to win. Jesus encourages us to find other ways to attain justice. I thought of this when I read about a young black man in a peaceful demonstration that turned violent during the Civil Rights Movement. He was attacked, kicked, and beaten bloody. At first he struck back at his attackers, but eventually he stopped doing so. He explained, "I realized I was only increasing the hatred. So I took their blows and hate into myself so it would go no further." This man lived to tell about his experience. Not everyone who refuses to return hate manages to do so. The church calls these persons *martyrs*.

When is it most difficult for you to not seek revenge?

Turning Toward Differences

Those who had diseases were pressing upon him to touch him.

Mark 3:10

People with all sorts of illness and disease reached out and pressed as closely as possible to Jesus in order to have physical contact with him. Think about that scene—the drainage and odor of open sores, the agonizing moans and pleadings of those with unbearable pain, the malformations of others with gut-wrenching maladies. Never once are we told that Jesus hung back or stepped aside because he felt repulsed by ill people who leaned against or touched him in order to be healed. Instead, he deliberately drew near and laid his hands upon them. I marvel at his extraordinary kindness and his ability to overcome any kind of hesitancy or revulsion. Think of how quickly we divert our eyes from someone with severe disabilities because we feel uncomfortable, or do not know what to say or how to respond. There is a natural tendency in us to ignore or withdraw from others whose mannerisms or appearance leave us feeling uncomfortable. Now is the time to ask our Compassionate Healer to help us turn our heart toward, rather than away from, the differences we prefer to avoid.

What physical differences cause you to stand at a distance instead of drawing near?

Untidy Healing

Putting spittle on his eyes, he laid his hands on him.

Mark 8:23

Why didn't Jesus simply say, "You're healed," or just place his hands on the blind man's eyes? One reason may be that some cultures considered spittle to have healing powers. I think there may also be a symbolic reason. Spittle is messy, intrusive, and considered disgusting to most people. Using spittle suggests that healing does not always happen in neat and tidy ways. Sometimes our spiritual healing arrives in forms that we resist because of the "spittle" in them. Such was the case when my religious superior reprimanded me long ago for my ultra-independence after I failed to ask permission for a significant decision I made by myself. Her admonishment hurt me, but eventually I saw the truth of what she said. This led me to reflect on my feelings of insecurity and to see my overcompensation of trying to care for everything myself. I didn't like the "spittle" of her comment, but it was a gift in that it caused me to modify my unhealthy attitude. I learned that God works through these experiences and helps us to heal and grow when "spittle" is thrust upon us.

How has "untidy healing" affected your life?

Upright of Heart

Light dawns for the just; and gladness, for the upright of heart.

Psalm 97:11

To be "upright of heart" suggests that my inner being stands in the solid peace that comes from living with integrity. If I listen and watch closely, I know when I am "upright of heart" and when I am not. I may be able to ignore not being upright for a while by rationalizing unpleasant behavior or unkind thoughts, but gradually my interior well-being jumbles up, becomes a tangle of negativity, and lacks goodwill. Eventually, I allow the Holy Spirit to help me understand how I am deceiving myself. The truth of what needs to change becomes apparent and urges me toward action. I have learned through the years how essential "daily discernment" is in order to detect this "distressing stew" that keeps me from being upright of heart. Most of the time this clarity reveals itself when I meditate or write in my daily journal. Then the interior falseness comes forth to greet me. If I am willing to face this duplicity and change what is required, joy and tranquility return to my spirit. Like the psalmist professes; Light dawns within me and gladness returns.

How "upright" is your heart today?

Waiting for Answers

**Your ways,
O Lord, make
known to me.**

Psalm 25:4

"I wish God would just tell me what to do." This comment came from someone struggling with a decision regarding a change of jobs. He was genuinely trying to make a decision compatible with what he thought God wanted for him. The desire to have the choice over and done with quickly by having the surety of God's preference is understandable. We long for fast answers. None of us likes to live with the anxiety of "what to do." Expectation of responses that have certainty or that will be quickly revealed are not realistic. Hearing a clear voice or receiving a definite "sign"—few people get to have this direct route in discernment. The "voice of God" is most often discovered gradually, through openness in prayer, deliberate stillness, the wise counsel of others, and going toward where the greatest peace lies amid the possible options. We are never without the Holy Spirit's assistance. Guidance and direction for our life continually await us. We find our decisions when we let go and allow God's revelation to quietly unfold, instead of pushing toward solutions that are not yet ripe.

*What solutions in your life
are not yet ripe?*

Where Do We Expect to Find God?

There was a tiny whispering sound.

1 Kings 19:12

The prophet Elijah follows the call to "go outside and stand on the mountain before the Lord." He trusts. He believes. He obeys. How surprised he is when the powerful episodes of nature—a wild wind that crushes rocks, an earthquake, and a sweeping fire—do not reveal the Holy One. Instead, Elijah is bowled over by the beauty of a "tiny whispering sound." This almost imperceptible murmur penetrates Elijah's heart, disarming him so much that he instinctively pulls his cloak around his face. This quick gesture speaks of both fear and wonder, an instinctual impulse to hide from what seems almost too powerful to experience. The small sound obviously seared the prophet's heart with a profound recognition of divine presence. Elijah's experience reminds me to not expect to find God in big stuff. Life is mostly composed of the tiny moments, the unnoticed sorts of things that hardly seem like divinity could be found there. I need to listen well throughout the day because there will probably not be wild wind and ominous thunder when the Holy One makes an appearance, only an elusive whispering sound like my own or another's breath.

Where do you expect to find the Holy One?

Who Will Be First or Last?

For behold, some are last who will be first, and some are first who will be last.

Luke 13:30

Nobody wants to be at the end of the line, whether it's the supermarket checkout or the entrance to a football game. I tend to respond with interior indignation when I am in line before others and someone else goes ahead. Something in me demands I have a right to be there. Jesus referred to this human response when he answered the question, "Will only a few people be saved?" The questioner thought only those who were religious and faithful to the law had a right to be in front, that they deserved to be there. Jesus responds by saying we may be surprised at who "will recline at table in the kingdom of God." It is not for us to judge worthiness. Our requirement is to check our reason for being morally good, upright individuals. Why do we participate in church and keep the commandments? Is it that we want to be "first in line," to get a place in the kingdom? Or is it that we activate our innate goodness out of love for God who continually invites us into a relationship that influences our behavior toward others?

How does the experience of being first or last affect your spirituality?

INDEX OF SCRIPTURE PASSAGES